ARTICLES

FOR THE

MIND

I0426502

58 Enlightening and

Objective Pieces of

Wisdom

CHRISTINE RICE

Articles for the Mind

By Christine Rice

© 2013 Christine Rice

All rights reserved.

ISBN-13: 978-1494277253

ISBN-10: 1494277255

Other books by Christine Rice:

Poetry for the Heart

Essays for the Soul

My Not-So-Ordinary Life

Freelance Writing Guide

Dedicated to my husband, who patiently and kindly accepted my lack of company during the eight months that I focused my attention on writing the articles found within.

Table of Contents

Foreword

This book contains 58 short nonfiction articles that are each broken up into small paragraphs to make them easy and enjoyable to read. The articles communicate a bounty of knowledge from my wide variety of numerous and significant life experiences. Some of the roles I've had that helped me provide the content for the articles, in no particular order, include: finance assistant, veterinary technician student, fashion merchandising student, freelance writer, caretaker to the mentally ill, retail clothing associate, mortgage refinancing telemarketer, health guru, organization perfectionist, loving wife and daughter, animal owner and lover, thrifty shopper, and environmental resources conserver.

This book can be read in any way you choose. It doesn't have to be read from beginning to end. It is grouped by category and alphabetically for your convenience, and for a sense of organization since there are a large variety of topics discussed. The information contained within these pages stems from my thorough research, education, and experience in the first three decades of my life. I wrote the articles with the purpose of informing you about the things I've learned in my life that I've found to be helpful, with the hopes that you will find some of it helpful too.

I hope you enjoy the readings in this book.

Sincerely,

Christine Rice

CHAPTER 1

BEAUTY AND HEALTH

The Benefits of Meditation for Relaxation

Relaxation is an important benefit of meditation, and everyone could benefit from relaxing more. Meditation is the best way to lessen stress, improve mood, and enhance sleep quality. It is helpful to know how the benefits of meditation for relaxation can improve a person's life so that you can decide if meditation is something you wish to pursue.

Less Stress

Many people breathe shallowly during the day. Shallow breathing does not help during times of stress and it can even hinder the situation further. However, when a person begins to meditate, he slows his breathing and takes deeper breaths. Quality breathing naturally relaxes a person because more oxygen, a necessary component of life, is absorbed by the body's cells and this helps the body and mind function better. And when the mind focuses on the body's rhythmic breathing, there are less thoughts and worries. Meditating once a day, and stopping to focus on and improve breathing quality periodically throughout the day (especially during stressful times), will decrease overall and acute stress.

Better Mood

The calming benefit of meditation improves mood. This is because meditation makes a person feel more peaceful, connected, and content. Meditation also helps "center" a person in the present moment. These positive sensations reduce worry, anxiety, and depression. When negative feelings are decreased, people have more room for positive feelings, such as optimism, hope, and happiness. Practicing meditation will improve a person's mood - not just during a meditation session but also throughout the day.

Improved Sleep Quality

Feeling more relaxed and less anxious during the day, from meditating once a day, will improve sleep at night. A person's sleep is better because of less stress and more positive emotions overall. Meditating helps a person fall asleep quicker, sleep deeper, and feel more refreshed in the morning. Meditating the following day will lead to better sleep the next night, and so on. Therefore, meditating every day will produce continuous improved sleep. Feeling more energized during the day, due to sleeping better at night, is an overall life benefit.

Meditation is a Beneficial Practice

Meditation clearly has mental and physiological benefits due to relaxation. The benefits are helpful to other areas of life, such as physical, social, and spiritual health. Meditation creates a chain reaction of positivity and peace in life that is priceless. It only takes ten minutes of mediation a day to reap the benefits. And meditation becomes increasingly more enjoyable and beneficial the more it is done. The benefits of meditation for relaxation make the time commitment well worth it.

The Best Snacks to Take on a Hiking Trip

Hiking is a great outdoor activity and form of exercise. Because of the exertion put forth, hiking requires you to have certain nutrients - proteins and complex carbohydrates - to supplement energy. Water is also a key ingredient needed for hiking to prevent dehydration. It is beneficial to refuel the body with these nutrients when you get hungry, whether it is before, during, or after the hike, or all three. The best snacks to take on a hiking trip that are forms of these important nutrients are: bananas, celery, peanut butter, and vitamin water.

Bananas provide a burst of energy from the natural sugar that is in it. This allows you to get substantial energy for the hike without consuming too much food. Less food, but those that will satisfy your appetite, like bananas, is best when physically exerting yourself. You will feel light and energetic to perform and complete the hike.

Celery is a healthy vegetable that provides substantial energy, because it is made of complex carbohydrates. It is also water-based and will satisfy thirst better than any other food. Celery is vitamin-enriched which makes it diminish your appetite. In addition, celery is very crunchy and requires lots of chewing, so it will satisfy your palate.

Peanut butter, especially if low in sugar, is a healthy power-food. The oil in peanut butter is made of healthy fats, which is good for brain and nerve function. The peanuts in peanut butter are a source of protein and carbohydrates, which makes it an effective energy-booster. And the salt in peanut butter replaces electrolytes that are lost through sweating, and draws water into the cells. These are all necessary functions for a hiking trip.

Water is a daily requirement. It is essential for getting rid of waste and helping organs to function properly. Vitamin water is a step up from water, because on top of getting hydrated, you are getting nutrients that your body needs. That will make you feel more energetic. You will also feel less hungry, because vitamin water curbs the appetite. It is crucial to be hydrated with water before the hike; take sips from a water bottle during the hike - especially at the midway point; and drink water after the hike, to rehydrate your body from all the activity.

When hiking, the body needs nutrients to replace those that are used. These nutrients are protein, complex carbohydrates, and water. Bananas, celery, peanut butter, and vitamin water best satisfy the required nutrients. If you consume these foods in appropriate amounts when you are hungry and thirsty on your hike, you will have a more enjoyable outdoor experience.

The Best Ways to Become a Healthy Eater— and Lose Weight too

An endless appetite, sedentary lifestyle, and unhealthy diet are far-too-often daily struggles for people. It is also usually difficult for them to lose weight and maintain weight loss.

These aspects of an unhealthy lifestyle are not easy to control and turn around, but it can be done! And fortunately, the ways to become a healthy eater are natural and help the weight loss process.

Eating Healthy Kills Cravings

The first step to becoming a healthy eater is to get rid of processed food and sugary beverages at home. Toss them out or give them away. Then fill up the cabinets and refrigerator with fresh fruits, a variety of vegetables, lean meats, low-sugar dairy, and lots of pure water. These nourishing foods will be better "fuel" for the body.

After just a few days of eating healthy, the desire to have junk food will decrease and the appetite will be more controlled. Because the body is receiving more nutrient-dense food, it won't be hungry all the time.

Cravings will diminish, but they may still occur occasionally. If they do, it is best to have a sugar-free/low-carbohydrate substitute, like gelatin, peanut butter, Greek yogurt, berries, etc. These foods will satisfy cravings without stimulating appetite or increasing body weight.

Eat Only When Physically Hungry

The second thing to work on is to satisfy physical hunger and avoid imaginary hunger. Physical hunger is the only true indication that the body needs nutrients. It is important to eat *every time* the body is physically hungry in order to keep appetite at bay and the metabolism working efficiently.

On the other hand, imaginary hunger is having an appetite for reasons other than the body needing energy—such as emotions, stress, lack of sleep, stimulated senses, and even thoughts. Whenever someone eats to satisfy imaginary hunger, they are overeating—it's that simple. And that means they will weigh more than they are supposed to weigh.

Eat Until Satiated, NOT Full!

It is still possible to overeat when only satisfying physical hunger—by eating past satiety. To avoid this, people should pay attention to how their stomachs feel when they are eating so they can stop eating when they are no longer hungry. It is not that easy. It requires slowing the process of eating **way** down.

It is important to stop eating when no longer hungry, because it takes approximately 20 minutes for food to reach the stomach and send a signal to the brain that it is full. So even though hunger is only satiated at first, in about 20 minutes the person will likely feel full.

Add More Physical Activity

Exercise helps control cravings and appetite by stabilizing blood-sugar. It also increases muscle mass, which decreases body fat, and that leads to a leaner—and often lighter—figure. Taking stairs, walking further distances, and stretching are physical activities that should be done regularly. Any amount of physical activity is better than none, of course, but moderate and consistent exercise is best.

Maintain Those Healthy Habits

A healthy lifestyle will become more innate, easy to do, and preferred with each successful day! It will also become easier to continue performing the new, healthy habits. Nutritious food will be favored because it satisfies the appetite better than junk food. And exercise may even become a welcomed and enjoyable routine.

Going from eating poorly and overeating, to eating nutritiously and correctly, will naturally result in weight loss. The amount and rate of weight loss will depend on:

1. How poor the eating habits were to begin with.
2. The degree and number of healthy changes made. Finally—it is important to maintain healthy changes to benefit most from them in the long run.

Common Myths about Calories

Calories are an energy source for the body. The body needs calories to perform voluntary and involuntary bodily functions. When lying still, the body still needs calories to perform respiratory, digestive, and circulatory functions. Therefore, the body cannot live without calories. However, there are certain myths about calories, in regard to dieting and weight loss, that people still believe in. These myths, and the real truths, are discussed below.

People are Overweight Because they Consume too Many Calories

There are many reasons why people are overweight, but the main cause is not from too many calories. Rather, eating sugary and processed foods leads to an increase in appetite and weight gain. That is because those types of foods quickly raise blood sugar levels and lower them just as quickly an hour or so later, leaving the person hungry soon after; and most of those foods have high fructose corn syrup and other unhealthy additives in them that the body gets physically dependent on and craves. If a person begins eating a greater number of healthy calories, as opposed to a lesser number of unhealthy calories, generally speaking, the person would not gain any weight and may even lose weight.

All Calories Affect Body Size the Same

All types of calories are not created equal. Sugary calories are quickly absorbed by the body in the form of glucose, which leads to the need for more sugar, because the spike in blood sugar creates a positive feeling that the body wants to repeat. However, eating sugary foods does not provide much, if any, nutrients to the body. Because the body is lacking nutrients, the person feels hungry shortly after and will eat again to obtain the nutrients it needs. It is a vicious cycle. Eating a majority of sugary calories will end up increasing body size. On the other hand, high-fiber calories take time to be digested and absorbed by the body, so the feeling of fullness lasts longer, the blood sugar levels remain fairly even, and the body gets the nutrients it needs so it is not hungry all the time.

Decreasing Calories Low Enough Results in Weight Loss

If calories are cut too low -- below 1200 a day -- the metabolism will slow. This is because the body needs to conserve calories in order to function and survive. A slowed metabolism means the body will not be as efficient at burning fat, and the person could get stuck at a plateau, or even gain weight. It is evident, then, that it would be a tough battle to reach and maintain a healthy weight if calories are cut significantly.

The Truth

If cutting calories doesn't result in weight loss, what does?

1. Eliminating, or greatly reducing, sugary and processed foods from the diet.
2. Eating a diet of mostly raw and fresh food, such as quality meats, fish, vegetables, fruit, and natural dairy.

3. Performing strength-training exercises; because muscle burns fat.

How to Become a Healthy Eater

Overeating is a common problem in society today. It often involves unsuccessful weight loss attempts and unhealthy eating. Food is not always easy to control though. Many people find themselves in a downward spiral when consuming unhealthy foods. Fortunately, there are ways to overcome unhealthy eating, limit overindulgence, and have lasting weight loss.

The first step is to become a healthy eater. Toss out or give away all foods and drinks at home that are processed (i.e. made mostly of sugar or flour). Go to the grocery store and buy fresh fruits, a variety of vegetables, lean meats, low-sugar dairy, and lots of pure water. Eating those types of foods will get the body used to running on healthy "fuel" and will stop the sugar dependency.

After just a few days, the desire to have junk food will decrease and the appetite will be more under-control. Because the body is receiving more nutrient-dense food and less sugar, it won't be hungry all the time.

Cravings will diminish, but they may still occur occasionally. If they do, it is best to have a sugar-free, low-carbohydrate substitute. This will satisfy the craving without stimulating appetite or increasing body weight.

The second thing to work on is satisfying physical hunger and avoiding emotional hunger. Physical hunger is the only true indication that the body needs nutrients and energy. It is important to eat *every time* the body is physically hungry to keep appetite at bay and the metabolism working efficiently.

Emotional hunger—having an appetite when the body doesn't need fuel—can also be thought of as imaginary hunger. Whenever a person eats to satisfy imaginary hunger, they are overeating. And that means they will weigh more than they are supposed to weigh.

It is still possible to overeat when only physical hunger is being satisfied. To avoid this, people should stop eating as soon as they are satiated, which is a sensation between hunger and fullness. However, it is not as easy as it sounds. It requires eating slowly and paying close attention to how the stomach feels.

It is important to stop eating when satisfied but not full, because it takes approximately 20 minutes for food to reach the stomach and send a signal to the brain that it is full. So even though hunger is only satiated at first, in about 20 minutes the person will probably feel full.

Exercise is a healthful activity that helps control cravings and appetite by stabilizing blood-sugar. It also increases muscle mass, which decreases body fat, and that leads to a leaner—and often lighter—figure. Taking the stairs, walking further distances, and stretching are physical activities that should be done regularly. Any amount of physical activity is better than none, of course, but moderate and consistent exercise is ideal.

A healthy lifestyle will become more innate, easy to do, and preferred with each successful day. It will also become easier to continue these new healthy habits. Healthy food will be favored, because it is more satisfying to the body than food with little nutrients. And exercise may become a welcomed and enjoyable routine.

Going from eating poorly and overeating, to eating nutritiously and correctly, will most likely result in weight loss. The amount and rate of weight loss will depend on:

1. How poor the eating habits were to begin with.
2. The degree and number of healthy changes made.

Finally, it is important to maintain healthy lifestyle changes to benefit most in the long run.

Low-Carbohydrate Diets are Best for Diabetes Management

When a person eats, the chemical, insulin, is produced by the body, in order to help regulate blood sugar, and is then absorbed by the cells. Generally speaking, this affects a person's energy levels and moods. However, the cells of people with type 2 diabetes do not receive insulin properly, so they are unable to regulate blood sugar. The best way to handle this is to cut out sugar from their diet (no sugar consumed means no need for insulin). Therefore, a low-carbohydrate diet is best for diabetics. Below is an explanation as to why that is so.

People with type 2 diabetes are not born with diabetes, but rather, they develop it later in life. It is believed that lifestyle, especially diet, affects a person's tendency to develop type 2 diabetes. More specifically, consuming a diet that is high in sugar and carbohydrates for many years can lead to type 2 diabetes. To reiterate, the cells of the person with type 2 diabetes cannot effectively receive insulin, and this is because the cell receptors are deformed from trying to receive too much insulin over the years.

Many people with type 2 diabetes take medication that sends additional insulin to the cells to help regulate blood sugar. However, the medication is unnecessary if sugar and refined carbohydrates are avoided. That is why the healthiest diet for people with type 2 diabetes is a low-carbohydrate diet. This is a diet that is low in sugar, which is a substance that is not necessary for proper body function, and which is harmful to the health of a person with diabetes.

Generally speaking, people who follow low-carbohydrate diets maintain normal blood sugar levels. In addition, not as much insulin is needed by the body because less sugar is consumed. This is what helps control diabetes. In fact, many people with diabetes who follow a low-carbohydrate diet, are able to take less medication (but only if instructed by their doctor).

The reason why a low-carbohydrate diet is better for diabetics, than simply a diet low in sugar, is because carbohydrates are converted to glucose quicker than protein-based foods, or other low-carbohydrate foods, like vegetables and cheese. And since glucose is a type of sugar, carbohydrates affect the body very similar to if sugar was consumed directly.

Some people with diabetes may worry about lacking the motivation to stick to a low-carbohydrate diet in the long-term. But many of them can still enjoy sugar-free deserts, snacks, and beverages, as well as some dairy products, nuts, and fruit. It is worth it for them to follow a low-carbohydrate diet as best as they can.

When people with type 2 diabetes follow a low-carbohydrate diet, the health benefits are incredible. If the diet is maintained for a significant amount of time, some people with diabetes are actually able to go off their medication (but only under the instruction and supervision of their doctor). Lowering medications and feeling better physically, are realistic goals for people with diabetes who eat a low-carbohydrate diet.

Pre-Makeup Skincare Tips

Taking care of your skin before applying makeup is very important, because skin serves as a "canvas" for the "artwork". If the skin is healthy and blemish-free, the makeup will look more pristine after it's applied. The following are several pre-makeup skin care tips to use for a beautiful face.

Wash Your Face Twice a Day, Everyday

Most people wash their face only once a day, such as in the morning when they take a shower before work. Like brushing your teeth, the face needs to be washed in the evening too. Imagine leaving makeup on overnight, along with air pollution and dirt accumulated on the skin, and how the pores will remain covered for an additional eight hours while sleeping. Skin needs to breathe, and removing dirt, oil, and makeup twice a day is necessary for healthy, clear skin.

Find the Right Facial Cleanser for Your Skin-Type

There is not one perfect facial cleanser for everyone, because not everyone has the same skin-type. There are many different products available at various stores. There are facial cleansers that remedy skin that is: blemished, dry, oily, red, aged, and a combination of them. You should shop around to try out various cleansers. And you don't need to spend a lot of money, because drugstores carry very good facial cleaners that are inexpensive, and there are also many generic products available that work just as good as the name brands. Eventually, you will be able to find a cleanser that has the best results for your skin and it will be worth it.

Always Remember to Exfoliate

It is very important to exfoliate the skin on your face every day. That is because it is easier for a face to glow when fresh skin is revealed. Exfoliating also helps to clear dirt out of the pores and remove and prevent bumps on the face. The easiest and most effective way to exfoliate is by using a non-smooth cloth material, such as a facecloth, soft pouf, sea sponge, or rough pouf (in order of softest to roughest) while washing your face. The degree of roughness of the exfoliating material you choose is up to you, and should depend on how sensitive your skin is. If, by chance, you do not like using a material to exfoliate, there are facial cleansers that have exfoliating beads in them that you can use, and the degree of roughness of the beads varies, so you are sure to find one that you like.

Use After-Cleansing Facial Products

Washing your face is not enough to properly care for your skin. There are additional products that are beneficial to use - such as pore strips, facial mask, toner, astringent, and moisturizer - depending on your skin-type. Pore strips can be used for the nose, chin, or forehead, and essentially remove the dirt and makeup that clogs pores. To use a pore strip, apply a little water to the skin and smooth the strip on. Leave the strip on for 10-15 minutes, and then slowly peel it off. It only needs to be done once or twice a week after cleansing.

Facial masks are helpful to produce radiant skin. They serve different purposes, but most deep-clean the pores on the face, even-out skin tone, and leave fresh, glowing skin. Depending on the type of facial mask, they should be applied daily to once-a-week. There are also facial cleansers that serve as facial masks if left on the skin rather than being washed off right away. Typically, masks should be left on the skin for 10-20 minutes. During this time, they usually harden and can then be peeled off or washed off.

Toner and astringent are recommended to clean the pores of blackhead and whitehead blemishes. Essentially, they get in crevices and deep-clean, which is very beneficial to most people. These products tend to dry the skin a little, so avoid using them on areas of your skin that are especially dry. Everyone can benefit from using a little toner, especially those with acne-prone skin.

Always use moisturizer in areas where your skin is dry. There are oil-free moisturizers for those who tend to get oily skin. Be open-minded when considering a moisturizer and flexible when applying it. For instance, you might not need to apply it liberally all over your face; you may just need to put a little on the driest areas.

There are lots of products and treatments that can be used to prep the skin before applying makeup. You don't need to use all of the after-cleansing products - just use the ones you like best that are most helpful for your skin type and purpose. And some of these products do not need to be used daily; in fact, some are recommended not to. But always remember to wash your face twice a day, and then apply other products as necessary. This routine will create and maintain fresh-looking skin that will be ready for makeup.

CHAPTER 2

CAREERS AND EDUCATION

10 Questions Job-Seekers Should Expect in an Interview

Being asked to come in for a job interview is an honor. It is your opportunity to represent yourself to a prospective employer. It is important to be aware of questions the interviewer is likely to ask, in order to be prepared to answer the questions during a time of stress. Ten of the most common interview questions are:

1. What can you tell me about yourself?

This is a question that requires a somewhat general answer. It is normally the first question asked in an interview because it opens the line of communication.

2. What Experience Do You Have Related to the Position?

This question asks you to list your skills, and past and present job duties. It is best to keep your answer focused, using keywords that are somehow related to the position you are interviewing for.

3. What Education do you have or Wish to Pursue?

Tell the interviewer several educational accomplishments, pursuits, and interests that you have. If possible, connect them to the position using similar keywords, or explicitly state how they are related.

4. What other personal and professional accomplishments do you have?

Here you can talk about more minor, but still important, achievements - such as promotions at work, helping others, or anything else you did that went above and beyond normal expectations.

5. What can you bring to the position if we hire you?

Your answer to this important question will tell the interviewer what you can do for the company, and your answer can make or break you. Think about the position itself - preferably done before the interview - and visualize how you would perform the job, then confidently state your answer.

6. What are your strengths?

Here the interviewer is interested in hearing adjectives that describe your personality. You can also state action verbs to show you are a go-getter and achiever. Try your best to relate it to the position.

7. What are your weaknesses?

The best way to answer this question is to state a challenge you have that you are overcoming or have recently overcome and explain how you've overcome it. The interviewer wants to learn how you handle negativity and setbacks because they are a part of life.

8. Give me an example of when you overcame an obstacle in your career.

Here you will give a challenge you had in the past and how you came out on top. It is best if the challenge was of medium intensity - not too difficult to explain, and not too simple that it will bore the interviewer.

9. How do you resolve conflicts in the workplace?

With this question, the interviewer wants to know how well you get along with others, how assertively you express your needs, and how much of a team player you are. Just be honest and tactful when you give an example - realistic or metaphorical - of a conflict that relates to the position and how you would, or did, handle it.

10. Why are you interested in working for us?

Doing previous research on the company is very helpful to answer this question. When researching, find out what the company does and its ethics. Tell the interviewer which aspects you share with the company.

Job interviews are tough. But being prepared, by knowing what questions will likely be asked, will help you perform better. You should also take preparation a step further by coming up with answers to the questions before the interview. This will lead you to having a successful interview.

5 Reasons to Quit Your Job

Most adults must work to live. But what if you hate your job? Some people feel trapped in their jobs even when the job negatively affects them. So how do you know when it's best to leave a job and find a new one? The following five circumstances are surefire reasons to quit your job.

1. You are Bored at Work

Maybe you've been working at the company for a long time and have reached a point where you cannot progress any further. The tasks have become mundane and you've literally memorized your job duties. Or you just started working for a company and have realized the position doesn't offer many challenges or much variety. Being stuck in boredom at work is depressing and may make you feel undervalued. If you are unable to transfer to a different position, or you don't see any opportunities for advancement, it is time to pack up and move on.

2. You Dread the Job

Something, or maybe a few things, about the job makes you dread going to work. Maybe it is your schedule, job duties, workload, coworkers, or boss. Whatever it is, it displeases you so much that you are miserable--before work, at work, and just thinking about work. The job is affecting your attitude: you lack motivation to do your work, you call in sick often, you arrive at work late and sneak out early, your mood is generally down, and you begin keeping to yourself. If you dislike your job so much that it affects your mood, actions, and attitude, you should be looking for a new job.

3. You are Being Harassed

"Office politics" is a common problem at many companies. People are social beings, so they gossip, choose sides, and form cliques--even at work. Unfortunately, some employees get picked on by their coworkers or boss. Being made fun of, being the brunt of mean jokes, being physically overpowered or assaulted, or receiving unwanted sexual advances are all reasons to report the situation and person who harassed you. However, often there needs to be multiple reports against a person before action is taken to correct the situation, and most people who are harassed aren't willing to wait that long for a solution. Being repeatedly harassed is a reasonable reason to quit a job.

4. The Job is Too Stressful

You're in a position where everyone dumps work on you, your boss has very high expectations, or your position is over your head. You're overloaded with work that is impossible to keep up with and it is only getting worse. You don't see yourself ever getting out of this predicament. You've tried talking to your boss and coworkers, but they say, "That's just the nature of the job." You stick around, trying your best to catch up with the workload, but the situation is not improving. There may be nothing else to do but to look for another job that is more rewarding and reasonable.

5. Your Health is at Risk

All of the reasons above may eventually affect your overall health if sustained long enough. There could be other reasons for poor health due to a job, such as performing physically challenging work when your body just can't handle it. Either way, it is always best to leave a job that is negatively affecting your health. Health is very crucial to happiness and wellbeing--and well, being alive--so if the decision is between a debilitating job and your health, you know which to choose.

Knowing when to quit a job is important for maintaining sanity, dignity, health, and happiness. When you see your situation at work is hopeless or heading downhill, start looking for another job immediately. You may be able to find new work in a reasonable amount of time so that your finances won't be affected much. Don't wait for your situation at work to get so bad that you must leave without having financial backup. And don't be timid or afraid to look for a new job. Believe in yourself and move on when necessary.

Hindsight: How People Want to Learn 'the Hard Way'

The most effective way to learn is through experience, and that is the method by which most people learn. It is very difficult to learn a lesson without experiencing any consequences. This is because information is best obtained and understood from live experiences. An example of this, is learning how to use a microscope: a person can be thoroughly instructed on how to operate a microscope, but until the person actually does it, he or she will not completely grasp the mechanics of it. In fact, many skills in life cannot be thoroughly understood until they are put to use or experienced. That is why many people must learn 'the hard way.'

Experience is the best teacher. Life lessons help shape people's values and belief systems. Unless life is lived, knowledge will not be understood, or absorbed in memory, to the fullest extent. This is why many people need more than verbal instructions to remember information. Demonstrating knowledge through action clarifies the message and ingrains it into memory. Only information that is remembered is actually learned.

The most effective lessons are often learned when people reach a 'bottom,' or utmost low point in his or her life. Jails, hospitals, rehabilitation clinics, and other facilities are examples of where people hit a bottom. At this point, hopefully they decide a change is in order. They must do something different, something positive, in order for their life to improve. And often, this is enough motivation for them to change. Bottoms are different for each person, and they can worsen if ignored.

Fortunately, most people do not hit a bottom in their lifetime. The majority of people learn from minor mistakes, enough that they do not choose to continue on the same path. However, sometime people need reminders of life lessons - reminders of what was learned from the prior experience to 'make sure' of the results - by repeating it.

People have different ethics and personalities so they act differently when faced with life circumstances. Some people are really careful to avoid mistakes; some are risk-takers; but most fall somewhere in between these two points. Like previously stated, the most effective way to learn is through action by trying out the experience. It is okay to try new experiences, make mistakes, and learn lessons. This is the most thorough way to grow as a person. It should be comforting to know that, most of the time people make good judgments, and most of life is neutral, not bad, experiences. It is not necessary to be afraid of making mistakes, or be ashamed for learning 'the hard way.' It is all a natural part of life.

How to Deal with Rejection while Job Hunting

Rejection is part of the job hunting process. You are not going to get every job that you apply to or interview for. This is because there is always more than one person applying and interviewing for a job, and often only one person will get hired. This is unfortunate, but is the way the job market works. That is why it is important to handle rejection with composure, take what you can from the experience, and continue applying.

Stay Positive

The most important thing, as far as your outlook on job hunting, is to keep a positive attitude. Job rejections happen all the time and you must expect them. So, try not to let them get you down. Think of the other opportunities that may be coming your way. And remember that you will eventually snag an opportunity if you keep a positive attitude. In general, you will find you get more positive results if you remain optimistic.

Keep Applying

Above all actions, do not stop applying because you got turned down. That is last thing you should do. Rather, when you do not get a job opportunity, look for another opportunity and apply to it. In fact, it is best to apply to several at a time to be more efficient. You don't want to hold all your hope on one opportunity. By applying to several you may avoid the disappointment from single rejections. So, keep applying until you are successful at obtaining a job.

Learn from the Rejection

With all experiences in life, it is beneficial to learn lessons from them. That way you can move on in a positive light and grow, which also leads to better outcomes. With job hunting, you could kindly ask the company what you could have improved upon or why they did not choose you. Or you could decide on your own what you think you could have done better - with your resume, cover letter, interview, or follow-up call or email - and do the more favorable action the next time. You will have more successful results with your job search if you learn from past experiences.

Summary

Learning from your actions and continuing on with a positive attitude will make you feel better and will help your job search results. Ultimately, persistence will lead you to get a job; so keep your chin up and keep trying. Also remember that there are other job seekers out there going through the same challenges as you. Eventually you will get the job that is right for you.

How to Spot a Dead-End Job

Jobs are a part of life for most adults. Usually, there are ways to advance to higher-paying positions within a company. However, occasionally you will find yourself in a job with nowhere to go, literally. It is important to be able to spot these positions so that you can make the best decision of staying or leaving.

Very low pay is a sign of a job with no growth opportunities. Positions at gas stations, fast food restaurants, and retail establishments do not promote often. Because there are significantly more workers than managers, the chances of advancement are slim. Not all low-paying jobs are dead-end prospects though, so you must consider other circumstances before making a final determination on the job's potential.

Sometimes there will be no jobs above you, because your position at the company is unique. In these cases, it is not easy to get promoted. For instance, you obtain a job that is one-of-a-kind, important even, and you put effort into learning the job well. (An example of this is an automobile sales person.) Eventually, you may come to the realization that the job leads to nowhere, because there are no higher-paying positions related to the work you do. In another scenario, you may even be the only person in the department, as is the case with some smaller companies. Therefore, it is best to look around and determine if there are growth opportunities with your position. If not, you must decide if putting in effort to excel at the company is worth your time in the long run. This analysis will help you decide on the path your career will take.

Some jobs have no avenue for promotion. In addition to the previous two situations mentioned (low-paying positions or unique positions), several factors may be involved: the position may be so specialized that it is hard to fill, and therefore, hard to get out of; the position is vital to daily production and profit, so it must be occupied all the time; or, the position has too many work duties that makes it too difficult, as well as highly inconvenient, to train new people for the position. In these cases, once in the position, the supervisor will not allow you to advance. In fact, if you are persistent about your superiors considering you for a different position, the company may even say you can leave if you are dissatisfied with your position, as a form of reversed-psychology, to try to make you stay.

Another good indicator that there is no way for you to advance at a company, is if your superiors do not appreciate the work you do. If they are dissatisfied with the quality and quantity of your work, they will not consider giving you a promotion. As a consequence of poorly viewed work, you may actually get demoted or fired. Therefore, if your work is not valued, at best you will remain in your position, and if you do not wish to stay where you are, you will have nowhere to go but down or out. The only thing you can do to improve your superiors' opinions of your work is to strive to do better. Find out their expectations, and try to achieve or surpass them.

If you want to advance at a company, the first thing you must do is learn your job well, and discreetly bring it to your supervisor's attention. If they notice you've excelled and they value your work, you will likely be considered for a promotion or increased salary. However, if there is no way for you to advance from your position, or your supervisor doesn't like your performance, it may be best for you to find a job that has better opportunities and is more fitting for your skills and personality. Being aware that a job is a dead-end position from the beginning is beneficial for your career path and future.

How to Write a Resume

Resumes have numerous sections in which to provide job-related information. There are various ways to arrange the different sections of a resume and various combinations of sections that can be used. Some possible sections are: objective, skills summary, skills, work experience, work history, education, languages, achievements, accomplishments, certificates, and work ethics.

It is crucial for a working adult to have a resume. It is the conversation starter for showing a prospective employer your skills and that you are interested in a job. There are certain basic steps every individual must take to create a resume from scratch.

1. Find a Position of Interest

It is important to have a job you are interested in to tailor your resume to. Choose a position you are qualified for. Print the details of the position if you prefer.

2. Gather Necessary Information

Certain information must be gathered in order to accurately and completely compose the resume. This information includes: a list of schools and dates of program completion for degrees and certificates; a list of employers, titles, and dates of present and past employment; and a list of computer programs and skills that you are experienced with. By compiling this information beforehand, the resume will be easier to complete in one sitting.

3. Create the "Objective" Section

Every resume must have an "objective" section. Write an objective using the job title of the position of interest. For example, most people start objectives with "To obtain a position as _____ ...." Personalize it, and add your own additional details, which could describe the type of company you wish to work for, the skills you can offer, or a combination of the two. It is always best to show the company what you can do for them if they hire you.

4. Develop a "Skills Summary"

Below the objective it is effective to put a concise list or description of your main job skills. Very rarely do managers have time to read an entire resume, because they have a stack of other resumes to review as well. So the skills summary will provide the most important information in the beginning to help the manager decide quickly whether you are qualified for the position.

5. Write the "Work History" and "Education" Sections

Next, provide the "meat" of your resume, which is your work history and education. Using the lists you previously compiled, start with your present or most recent employer and work your way back in time, writing the business name, location, dates of employment, and job titles. Do the same for education, but instead use: school name, location, date of graduation (or dates of attendance), and degree type and name. You can decide which section - work history or education - will go first based on how relevant the information is to the position and the level of importance of the information.

6. Create the "Experience" or "Skills" Section

You can choose to tie your experience and skills into the work history section. However, a long list of skills and experience should have its own section to make the resume more balanced. Whichever you choose, you should list your experience and skills using phrases that begin with action verbs, and maintain parallel sentence and word structure throughout. Group the skills and experience into categories, such as computers, manufacturing, retail, management, and so on, to keep the list organized and easy to follow.

7. Make Lists for "Achievements" and "Work Ethics"

Lastly, write separate lists of your accomplishments and work personality traits under the headings of "achievements" and "work ethics." Name your work and personal accomplishments and well-rounded, mostly professional, personality traits. These sections effectively wrap up the resume and have the ability to leave a positive impression with the prospective employer.

Final Words

The resume is now complete. Type it and format it with the word processor, using various formatting options to make it pleasant to read. Read it through several times. You can also have a colleague evaluate it to let you know if there is anything they recommend changing. If you followed the previous steps, you are sure to have an organized, substantial resume that will hopefully get your foot in the door to a great company.

Maturity at Work as a Tool to Keep Moving Forward in Your Career

Being mature at work is beneficial for everyone. It helps a company operate smoothly by maintaining workflow, increasing productivity, and improving employee cooperation. Most importantly, it will earn a company more money. Therefore, mature employees are valued by upper management and, consequently, they will move up in their careers at a faster rate.

On the other hand, immature employees gossip, get behind in their work duties, cause disputes in the office, disrupt other employees, slow workflow, and generally cost a company significant money due to their negligence. If a company was made of all immature employees, the company would fail.

Hence, maturity in the workplace helps a company succeed. When a company succeeds, upper management is very pleased. They can tell the mature employees are producing higher quality and quantity of work, making decisions to help the company prosper, and helping the work environment function smoother.

That is why mature employees are getting more promotions and doing so at quicker rates.

The following are some examples of how maturity helps a company thrive and why it would help an employee to prosper in their career.

Maintaining Workflow

Mature employees work continuously; they are always doing something that will contribute to the organization they work for. They are at work to work, plain and simple. They keep a consistent and steady workflow with the tasks they do. Workflow that continues, and does not get backed up, is very helpful to a company. It is the reason the company is alive. Upper management notices employees who work constantly, and they will reward them with higher pay and positions.

Increasing Productivity

In addition to keeping the work moving along at a steady pace, maturity in the office increases work production. When an immature employee is replaced by a mature one, much more work will get done. The more productive employees are, the less employees that are needed, which saves a company money. This makes upper management very happy and they will compensate these employees with bonuses and promotions.

Improving Employee Cooperation

Mature employees communicate more effectively and have improved temperament, leading to employee cooperation and collaboration. This benefit is on a different level than workflow and productivity, because it has to do with human interaction, but it is also important for helping a company succeed. For example, an office of mature employees will get along better, have improved team functioning, and will have superior communication. This leads to less mistakes, higher quality work, and a more pleasant work environment.

These are all positive attributes that a company desires, so upper management will appreciate and give credit to those employees who make it happen.

Mature Employees Means Higher Company Worth

Clearly, maturity in the office means a higher-functioning and smoother-operating company. The company will make more money, just from a mature employee replacing an immature one. It is very important to be mature at work, to gain the respect of others and thyself, and those who are will be well-rewarded by upward movement in their careers.

An Overview of the Job Hunting Cycle

Job hunting is a continuous cycle that is well-known by most adults. The cycle starts in motion as soon as someone posts their resume, or looks at a job posting, or even just thinks about how it would be nice to have a new, different, or higher-paying job. There are several parts to the job hunting cycle.

Updating Your Resume and Cover Letter

Before applying to a job, or even thinking about applying, your resume and cover letter should be up-to-date, revised, and polished. It is best to have at least one main version that is ready to submit so that other versions can more easily be created when you begin applying to different jobs. You can update your resume yourself; ask a family member, friend, or colleague; or hire a professional resume writer. Either way, make sure all past and present work history, experience, education, and skills are included. You may need to update the "objective," if your goals have changed.

Searching for a Job

It is easy to stay on top of new job postings with the Internet and email. You can go to a couple of job websites, do several job searches, and save the best searches. Then make it so you will receive emails -- as often you want -- of the new jobs. It may take some time to initially set up the saved email searches, but the extra time spent is well worth the convenience of not having to plug in the search criteria each time. It is also a good idea to check out social networking websites for job leads and to let others know you are job hunting. There are also websites where you can post a professional profile so that employers will come to you.

Submitting Job Applications

Once you find a job that you would like to apply to, adjust your resume and cover letter accordingly -- you may even want to write a fresh cover letter and totally rework your resume. It's up to you and what you think the company would prefer. Once your resume, cover letter, portfolio items, and application are adjusted and read-over, you can submit your documents to the employer. Remember, you are selling yourself to a prospective employer that has certain requirements for the job application process, and if you can follow their guidelines correctly, it tells them that you can follow directions and are attentive -- two admirable traits. They will be impressed from the start.

Following Up on the Applications

One of the most important parts of obtaining a job is following up after applying. That is the time when companies receive a lot -- sometimes hundreds -- of applications, so a follow-up by email, phone, or letter is often necessary to obtain a job interview. A follow-up should be done within 7 to 10 days of the submission date, or sooner, if an online application was submitted (Quintessential Careers). Pick the method of follow-up that you are best at performing, and then do it; don't delay. You may find it efficient to create a spreadsheet of the companies you apply to along with places to check off when a follow-up is done. When you follow up with the company, be brief and polite. Help them to want to contact you back for an interview by suggesting it tactfully. Reflect your confidence about your skills, not how desperate you are for a job. Remind them of what you can do for their company. If you follow these suggestions, you have a good chance of getting your foot in the door.

Preparing for your Interview

Preparation is the key to a successful interview, and a successful interview is the key to a job offer. To prepare for an interview, do the following:

1. Research the company. You must be familiar with the company in order to sell yourself on what you can do for them. By doing a little research before the interview, you will best know how to answer their questions. That will show you already know your stuff and they will be impressed.

2. Write down questions you have about the company and the job. At the end of an interview, an interviewer always asks if you have any questions. When people encounter something new, they usually have questions about it. If you have 2 or 3 questions, it will show your interest in the position and company.

3. Put yourself in the prospective employer's shoes. What do they want to know about their job applicants? They will ask you general questions about yourself. Plan on making your answer relate, in a natural way, to your job skills and job performance. They will ask you questions about your past and present job duties. Be prepared to talk about what you do and what you know. Don't be afraid to boast about your accomplishments. If you're not presently employed, they will probably ask why. They will also

ask you about your strengths and weaknesses. Plan to say in your answer how the strengths relate to your work, and turn the weakness you give into a positive by showing how you have tackled it and grown from it.

4. Plan what you will wear, down to your shoes and accessories. Prior to the interview, drive to where the interview will be held so there will be no chance of getting lost or being late on the day of the interview. Set aside an extra hour to get ready in case of any unforeseen circumstances, and especially if you tend to underestimate how long things take you.

Attending the Interview

Be punctual for your interview -- approximately 10 minutes early is sufficient. Give a firm handshake and look your interviewer in the eye. Try your best to be polite, confident, and knowledgeable. Listen to your interviewer closely. They will be asking you questions, obviously, and if you listen well, it will be easy to provide answers and you won't get off track. It is good to give explanations and statements. Don't give a long story for an answer, because it may lead you to say the wrong thing, and you will be talking too much. Being pleasant, positive, and enthusiastic, and following the suggestions above, will give you a great chance of getting the job. Lastly, ask the interviewer for their business card for reference later, and remember to shake their hand at the end.

Following Up After the Interview

Just like there are many job applicants, there are many interviewees too. It is a good idea to follow-up with the interviewer, preferably by the following day. An email or phone call is best so that they will get the message soon. Let them know that you enjoyed meeting them and learning about the company. Tell them how interested you are in the job, and remind them of the important points of why you're perfect for the job.

Now you must wait for their decision. If it's a "yes," you're likely all set with job hunting for at least a little while. You can still keep your resume up-to-date as you acquire new skills, experience, and education. If the decision was a "no," it's time to continue the cycle. Not getting a job offer with your first interview is not a big deal, because most people don't. You'll get more interview practice and will be more skilled at obtaining a job. All adults have to perform the job hunting cycle at some point, and if you're aware of how to handle the parts, you will be a success.

The Role of Education and Knowledge in Today's World

Life is very fast-paced these days. Many people have to juggle work, school, family, and home. With the increase in time comes the need for an increase in knowledge.

Nearly all adults have some type of post-secondary education, whether it be trade school, certificates, associate's degrees, or more. And usually it is *much* more. Bachelor's degrees are now the average level of education for adults. As time progresses, the education required to comfortably survive in this world will too increase.

With the advancement of time comes the advancement in knowledge and technology. Scientists, doctors, researchers, and technicians discover new methods, organisms, facts, information, and terminology, to increase human knowledge. This leads to the ability to learn about additional valuable aspects of the world. Knowledge, like time, is vast and abstract, possibly never-ending.

Competition is at its peak in regards to people, colleges, and employment—and it's all because of education and knowledge. People compete for the highest-paying positions, the most productive workers, the largest salaries, the best schools, and the most compatible companions. We must have advanced degrees from prestigious colleges in order to get far. Liberal Arts majors and Associate's Degrees are no longer sufficient to live comfortably in today's society.

The process of obtaining education and succeeding in the workplace is more demanding and less rewarding, because there is very little time to relax. In fact, relaxing is now often compared to laziness and weakness. On the other hand, individuals who work overtime and skip their lunch breaks, or those who stay up unreasonably late to study for tests, are considered winning employees and exceptional students. That is likely so, but they are also exhausted and overwhelmed from their performance.

Increasing knowledge is a path that will continue for generations to come. Computers, the Internet, and cell phones allow people to more efficiently communicate and obtain information. There are virtual classrooms, instant messaging, online libraries, and so on—all within our reach.

As a society, we have evolved, and therefore, grown accustomed to these fast-paced living, working, and learning conditions. Although, there are still positive aspects of it. Gaining knowledge is fun and liberating and, because we are all subjected to the world and able to learn, we can gain knowledge about anything we desire.

Education may be more advanced now, but *all* aspects of life are more complicated. Society and education can only be compared to the time in which it was experienced.

Setting the Scene for Success in Adult Education

Having a college degree is now a commonplace achievement for adults. Increasingly advanced degrees are becoming necessary for job seekers to obtain positions in their career fields. Therefore, many adults return to college in order to meet or exceed educational standards. In addition, competition for jobs has grown rampant with the ongoing economic struggles. This competition, and the need to prosper, is why adults are deciding to continue their educations.

It is not easy for adults to return to college, because most of them have been away for years and are already settled into their home lives and work situations. An effective way for adults to return to college and be successful, is to first consider personal strengths and weaknesses, and then decide on the best strategy to accomplish their goals. Strategies can differ depending on the person. Managing time, increasing productivity, and getting tutoring are some techniques to consider.

It is helpful to realize that there are certain personal attributes that help adults succeed at their studies: motivation, ambition, and determination. Motivation is needed to have the desire to return to school. Then, ambition helps move along the process of deciding to enroll and completing the enrollment process. Without motivation and ambition, enrollment would not happen. The positive feeling of motivation, intertwined with the act of ambition, sets the scene for a successful educational future.

Motivation is clearly necessary when obtaining an education. Students need motivation nearly every day in order to participate in class discussions, review the assigned readings, accomplish assignments, and pass each class. Motivation is what will carry an adult student through their classes - one class at a time - until completion. There are ways to help maintain the feeling of motivation:

1. Review long-term goals.
2. Learn about jobs that will become an option after graduation.
3. Get involved in extracurricular activities related to the educational goal.

Determination is needed to overcome obstacles that can interfere with program completion. While in attendance, students may experience depressing and difficult moments, times when inspiration or interest is lacking, and life issues that occur and take away their focus. Having determination will get them through those tough times. It is what will help them go over the finish line to earn their degree.

Determination is clearly necessary for a student to graduate. With determination, nothing will stop the student from obtaining their goals.

Having a strategy to tackle personal weaknesses, and maintaining motivation, ambition, and determination, are important for success in adult education. When a person discovers why they want to further their education, they will start to develop the attributes necessary for success.

Signs you are in the Wrong Career

Careers are an elaborate topic. Some people spend their entire lives searching for the perfect line of work. Others think work is supposed to be difficult and straining—that's why it's called "work." So how do you know if you're on the wrong career path? There are three aspects of yourself to consider when deciding on your perfect career field: Your attitude, your motivation, and your interests.

In regards to attitude, think about your moods, not just during work, but also before and after. Are you generally happy or cranky? How do you feel every morning when you think about facing the workday? What is your mood like during work? What kind of attitude do you have about your job? How do you feel after work? These are all important questions to reflect upon when trying to decide if you are in the wrong career.

Most people's jobs affect their entire lives, and this is especially noticeable when it is an unfitting job. If your job makes you feel angry, depressed, frustrated, or overwhelmed for extended periods of time, you should probably look for another job. Your attitude portrays how you truly feel about your job and it cannot be denied. Therefore, a negative attitude is the first sign of being in the wrong career.

If your motivation at work is low and your job duties do not appeal to you, then you are clearly not interested in what your job entails. This is a sure sign your career is not right for you. As stated before work affects home-life, so also having low motivation outside of work means your job is draining you. People who feel completely worn-out from their jobs do not enjoy what they do, because no one gets worn-out from doing things they enjoy. Therefore, a significant lack of motivation and energy deems an unfit career.

Your interests are the key to realizing how fitting—or not—your career is. Determine what you enjoy based on your hobbies and things you like. Say, you like the arts, such as painting, acting, and writing, but your job is in Finance. Evidently, you are going against the true grain of your personality. If you are performing work that you wouldn't choose to do in your spare time, then your job may not be a match for you.

Discovering your interests and building upon them is the first step to realizing your fitting career field. But first you must start by evaluating your attitude and level of motivation. It takes a little introspection and insight but it's not too difficult. Pretty soon you'll be on your way to finding the perfect career.

Signs You Need a Career Change

Careers involve a lot of thought and attention. This is especially true if you are not happy with yours. It may be called "work," but that doesn't mean you need to feel miserable.

Some people spend their entire lives searching for the perfect job. What they may not realize is that it may not be the particular job that is unfit, but rather the line of work. If you've been wondering lately if you're on the wrong career path, there are three things to think about when considering a career change: your attitude, your feelings, and your motivation.

Attitude is a Reflection of Your Career

Your attitude about your career reflects how fitting, or not, it is. You may want to reflect on the following questions: What is your attitude about facing the workday? What outlook do you have about your career? How do you view your work environment and colleagues? These are important questions to think about when deciding if a career change is in your future.

Feelings are Revealing

Because a career usually takes up a considerable amount of time of a person's life, how they feel, both on and off the job, represents their career's effect on them. If you feel angry, depressed, frustrated, or overwhelmed for extended periods of time, you should probably look for another career. Your feelings portray how you truly feel about your career and they cannot be denied. Therefore, consistent negative feelings are a sure sign of being in a wrong career.

Lacking Motivation = Unfit Career

If your motivation at work is low, and your job duties do not appeal to you, then you are clearly not interested in what your career entails. This is a definite sign that it is not the right match for you. Experiencing low motivation at home as well can mean your job is draining you. Those who feel completely worn-out from their jobs typically do not enjoy what they do, because people rarely feel depleted of energy from doing things they enjoy.

Finding Your Perfect Career

Identifying your interests is the first step to selecting the right career. Start by making a list of your hobbies, and then come up with a career field where you could apply one or more of your passions. It may take a little introspection, but the prospect should feel more natural to you. Pretty soon you'll be well on your way to enjoying a new career!

What Hiring Managers Look for In a Job Interview

A job interview is the perfect time to show off your professional skills and personality. An interview is your one opportunity to make the right impression to the hiring manager. They will evaluate you on various personal and professional traits. The following information discusses the traits that hiring managers will look for in you as an interviewee.

Neat Appearance

The very first aspect of you that the interviewer will notice is your appearance. It is commonplace for an interviewer to evaluate your appearance. Most want to see professional attire that is unwrinkled and clean, a fresh-looking face and hands, and appropriate hair in a style that looks professional. They don't want to see overdone makeup, dirty nails, or old shoes. Make sure you and your clothes are clean and neat and you will be evaluated highly.

Confident Body Language

Your body language speaks louder than your words. The hiring manager can tell a lot about you by your posture, mannerisms, and body positions. They will be impressed if you have straight posture, present yourself confidently, and position your body in a friendly and welcoming way. It is best to look natural but not sloppy. Practice interviewing with a colleague, while focusing on your body language, and you will see where you can improve.

Aim for body language that says you are a confident professional.

Clear Eye Contact

The most effective way to connect with hiring managers is to have natural eye contact. It reveals that you are interested, confident, and honest. If you make a good connection with the hiring manager, they will want to hire you. Also, making eye contact often will give you a better perspective on the interview so that you will be able to act appropriately.

Professional

The hiring manager will evaluate you on your level of professionalism based on how you look, how you express yourself, and how you share your successes, just to name a few. Professionalism is impressive to hiring managers and reveals a lot about you. It implies that you are confident, successful, ambitious, and intelligent. Most hiring managers want to hire someone who is professional. To act professionally, do your best to share information in an appropriate way and be straightforward about your accomplishments. If you do, the hiring manager will likely want you to work for them.

Effective Communicator

Being an effective communicator will surely impress the hiring manager and will convince them that you are the right candidate for the job. If you express your talents and accomplishments, and state what you can do for the company, the hiring manager will think highly of you. Effective communication is very important and will be one of the deciding factors when the hiring manager chooses who to hire.

Compatible with the Company

The hiring manager probably has already reviewed your resume, so they are not as interested in you reiterating the information to them as they are in you telling them interesting facts about you and your professional past. Tell them things about you that aren't on your resume, like your goals, ambitions, and accomplishments. Sharing with them will allow them to decide if your personality will fit in with the company.

Job interviews are not easy. In fact, they can be highly stressful. To make the interview go easier, be prepared for the situations mentioned above, and practice and plan out the interview. By putting your best foot forward and reflecting the above traits in the job interview, you will likely satisfy the expectations of the hiring manager and will have a good chance at getting hired.

Where to Find Entry-Level Sustainability Office Jobs

Sustain - the root word of sustainability - means "to keep up or keep going, as an action or process." Office jobs are sustainable for people who enjoy computer work, paperwork, and helping others. Entry-level jobs are often not sustainable; rather, they are beginning opportunities for getting a foot in the door of a company with hopes of other positions opening up or getting a promotion. So, where does a person obtain a sustainable entry-level office job? The following types of offices have them, but the level of sustainability of the job also depends on the person's interests.

Doctor or Dentist Office

If the person looking for an entry-level job likes to help people, feels comfortable interacting with others, enjoys sitting most of the time, likes filling out paperwork, and is skilled with computers, a position as a receptionist in a doctor or dentist office is perfect. This is an entry-level job for the right candidate. Some people who work in this type of position get to know, and get along with, almost everyone, so the coworkers and patients become like a second family to them. Some medical receptionists enjoy the new skills they learn. And many remain in the job for years.

Insurance or Finance Office

Is the job seeker good with math? Does he or she like organizing paperwork? If so, a position as an office assistant in insurance or finance would be fitting. Some insurance companies also need customer service representatives and receptionists, so if the person is apt at communicating technical information to a less-knowledgeable person, the potential employee would be qualified for the position and would excel at it. Financial and accounting offices also hire entry-level data entry clerks and file clerks, so those who are computer savvy, or enjoy maintaining organization, would be happy to stay in those positions.

Retail Office

People who are interested in fashion and merchandise, are good at conversing on the phone, like to sort paperwork, enjoy using computer programs, and take pleasure in helping others, would find it pleasing to work as an entry-level administrative assistant in a retail office. Administrative assistants are receptionists that also assist someone from upper-management. While working for their supervisor, an administrative assistant answers the telephone and directs calls, types letters and enters data into the computer, maintains an organization of files, and greets and helps visitors that come to see his or her supervisor. This is an ideal job for someone who is confident, polite, helpful, and hardworking.

Sales Office

There are often telemarketers, who call potential customers to sell a product or service, in a sales office. These are entry-level positions made for assertive, friendly, good communicators. Usually telemarketers handle a lot of paperwork or computer work or both. Sales offices have lots of paper files where applications, invoices, and records are kept. Telemarketing for a sales office is a good position for a person who enjoy sales, namely being persuasive and convincing, and talking to people on the telephone Those who stand for the product or service being sold, find their jobs most rewarding.

There are probably many other types of offices that have entry-level positions. In fact, almost all offices require entry-level employees to handle the less-challenging work. Some people enjoy easy work and an office environment, so they would find any office position sustainable

CHAPTER 3

FAMILY AND PETS

Dealing with the Ups and Downs of Married Life

Marriage naturally comes with ups and downs because it is imperfect, like life itself. Some married couples only expect the ups, and are therefore not prepared for the downs. It is essential for married couples to be aware of the rollercoaster of emotions that comes with most marriages. Fortunately, there are various ways to handle the ups and downs of married life.

Make Responsibilities Fair and Equal

The couple should take a look at what each person does with their time. They should consider work, school, chores, kids, church, and other concrete responsibilities. Then, they should adjust the responsibilities just enough so that the time and effort of the responsibilities is equal. Also they should take into account the degree of pleasure or displeasure involved with each responsibility in order to make sure the responsibilities are fair. A good approach is for the couple to first figure out what responsibilities each person likes best, give those to the correct person, and then divvy up the remaining responsibilities. Fair and equal responsibilities will make a married couple happier and more civil.

Make Time for Togetherness

The quality time a couple has together is very important for their love to grow. People naturally grow and change as individuals, but quiet times together hold marriages together. Togetherness makes it hard for couples to be mad at each other. It also keeps the love connection between a married couple united over the years. Plus, each person likely has their own career and activities to tend to the majority of the time, so if they get together daily to reconnect with each other, by sharing the events of the day and watching a movie or having dinner together, they will have a loving, long-lasting marriage.

Create a Budget and Stick to it

Finances are one of the most fought about topics in a marriage. It is disturbing for couples to keep fighting about the same things over and over again. It is best to try to resolve the issue. Creating a household budget, and sticking to it, of course, is an effective way for couples to deal with financial disagreements, as well as keep finances in check. A budget should include all sources of income, all expenses, savings plans, and investment plans. Nothing should be left out and expenses should be round up so there will be no surprises. It is helpful to record in the budget who is responsible for each section and to make sure the budget is mutually agreed upon. Then, the budget should be followed accurately, and if a financial issue arises, they can refer back to the budget together. It will create a sound marriage.

Take Fights Lightly

Fighting is about events and situations. It is not about the love between couples. Therefore, fights are not personal. If fighting is viewed that way, fights will not appear to be the end of the world when they happen. In fact, fights happen occasionally for all married couples because people are human. A fight should be thought of as simply that - a fight. It is a mere disagreement based on opinions and perspectives. No one is right all the time and perspectives are subjective, so both people have legitimate reasons for their thoughts and behavior no matter how right they each think they are. In other words, it is best for people to put themselves in the other person's shoes to be more understanding of their viewpoint. Then the fight will be over quicker and their lives will resume more civilly.

Learn from Arguments

The best thing a couple can do at the end of an argument, is discuss what each person has learned from it. The argument happened and the couple is back to being civil again, but they would benefit more from gaining a moral lesson from the dispute. What did they each learn about the other person during the argument? What is the best way for them to handle what they fought about if it happens again? And most importantly, how can they avoid the bad situation from happening again? If couples don't gain something helpful from an argument, it is entirely a negative and upsetting situation. Something, even if just minor, must change, or else it will happen again, almost guaranteed. Usually a couple is happy when an argument is resolved and they want to avoid the negative topic entirely. But, discussing the argument maturely, while it's still fresh, is a good idea for couples to prevent the situation and argument from happening again.

Love Each Other Unconditionally

Married life needs love to work. Spouses loving each other is the main reason that a marriage remains together. Unconditional love is complete love for someone for who they are as a person. That means they do not have reservations or other feelings confused with love. Unconditional love creates a sturdy marriage. Marriages can be rocky at times, but if there is unconditional love, there will be a rope connecting the couple together so they won't leave each other. It is important for married couples to show their unconditional love by being kind and affectionate to each other. Showing love makes the bond of marriage even stronger.

Final Words

Marriages require a lot of effort and responsibility. There are ups and downs, good days and bad days, and loving moments and mad moments. That is what a marriage is made of because that is life. However, it can be a mostly enjoyable experience if handled with fairness and love. Not only will the good times be treasured, but the bad times will be helpful learning experiences that will bring the couple closer together. By dealing with the ups and downs, married life will be a treasure.

Habits of Happily Married Couples

Many couples have happy marriages. Depending on the spouses' personalities, being happily married comes easy to some, and takes work and effort for others. All spouses can have happy marriages if certain habits are followed.

Be Understanding of Each Other's Flaws

People, as we know, are imperfect. Rather than be critical of each other's mistakes, happily married spouses are compassionate and understanding of each other. This means they are patient and accepting of each other as individuals. This also means they accept each other's flaws. Some happily married spouses love each other's imperfections, because imperfections make people unique. Being understanding and accepting naturally encourages spouses to get along better. And getting along is a very important aspect of a happy marriage.

Help out Equally

In a happy marriage the spouses are on the same "team." This is because marriage is a partnership of two people in love, and a happily married couple remembers that and withholds that belief. It is much easier for two spouses to live together happily if they are on each other's side and work together. This means putting in equal effort in all areas of the marriage and household, willingly.

Agree to Disagree Sometimes

Effective communication is an integral part of a happy marriage. Occasionally, spouses' opinions will differ.

For minor issues, no happily married spouses need to force one to take the other's side, completely, 100% of the time. This is because some conflicts are just differences in opinion. Since there are many viable opinions in the world, sometimes spouses should agree to disagree; meaning, both spouses will accept that they disagree on an issue and that is okay. Rather than fight about the small stuff, they let each other have their own opinions and individuality. They also embrace each other's unique traits.

The Secret to Happy Marriages

Happy marriages usually take work. Sometimes occasional heart-to-heart discussions are necessary to get back on the right track. Respecting each other's differences in personality and opinion is important for any two people that live together. As well, putting in equal effort in all areas of a marriage creates a strong, long-lasting marriage. In addition, happily married couples have a little secret: they focus on doing all they can to get along the best that they can. Lastly, happily married spouses are understanding, helpful, and accepting of each other's differences. And now the secret to a happy marriage is out!

How to Maintain a Close Mother-Daughter Relationship

Mothers and daughters have a special connection. It can be a close relationship where they are good or best friends. It can also be a difficult relationship where their personalities conflict. There are, however, ways for mothers and daughters to remain close. Those ways are: keep in touch often by phone, share gifts and cards in the mail, visit in person as much as possible, share personal information, and show affection.

Keep in Touch Often by Phone

When mothers and daughters are apart for significant amounts of time, it is important to keep in touch by phone. They should both give effort to call one another occasionally, once a week or more, depending on the circumstances. This allows them to stay updated on each other's lives - both the good and the bad. They can discover solutions to problems, enjoy funny moments, and share good and bad news. Talking on the phone is a good substitute when they cannot get together in person.

Share Gifts and Cards in the Mail

When mothers and daughters live in different locations, such as different states or countries, sending and receiving gifts in the mail allows them to appreciate each other without being together. This way, they are able to keep in touch on holidays, birthdays, and anniversaries. Then they won't miss sharing special occasions with each other. They can also be pen pals and share their lives with each other through mail. Gifting and writing each other can also be done electronically. These are ways for them to show they care and are thinking of each other when they can't be together.

Visit in Person as Much as Possible

Phone calls and sending mail are great ways to maintain a close mother-daughter relationship, but it is additionally helpful to see each other and spend time together as much as possible. Oftentimes, the more visits they share, the closer their relationship will be. This is because, being in the presence of each other allows for the most closeness and ability to connect. Mothers and daughters can bond best when they share each other's company. Times spent together, no matter how often, will increase the closeness of their relationship.

Share Personal Information

For mothers and daughters to remain close, they should share their personal experiences, thoughts, and beliefs with one another. It is fine to talk and laugh about daily events, but also talking about deeper feelings helps draw them close. This is because, when they open up to each other, they can bond and connect by being supportive, caring, and understanding. Each will feel honored that the other person trusts them enough to confide in them, and this will strengthen their relationship.

Show Affection

It is important for mothers and daughters to show they love each other in order to maintain their close relationship. Affection often brings people closer together. Mothers and daughters can show affection however they feel comfortable. They should not force affection, but initiating affection can allow for more easily affectionate moments. Giving a hug or saying how they feel about each other are great ways to show affection. These intimate moments will create and maintain closeness between a mother and daughter.

Remain Close over the Years

Mothers and daughters have great potential for close relationships. This is because females tend to be more open and loving than males. By keeping in touch often, sharing person moments, and showing occasional affection, a mother-daughter relationship is sure to remain close for years to come.

How to Meet the Outdoor Needs of Your Indoor Cat

Simply stated, indoor cats have special needs because they don't go outside. These needs are: playing, fresh air, and freedom. It is important to meet these needs so that your cat will be happy and fulfilled.

Cats Need to Hunt

According to National Geographic, "Like their wild relatives, domestic cats are natural hunters able to stalk prey and pounce with sharp claws and teeth." However, indoor cats don't have prey to hunt, just your occasional insect, so they are unable to satisfy their natural hunting instinct.

There are various ways to satisfy your cat's need to hunt. You can give them battery-operated cat toys, that symbolize rodents and birds, to play with. You can also provide your cat with flexible strings that hang from the ceiling, balls that roll easily across the floor, and toys that make noises when moved or pounced on.

Or, you can repeatedly move stationary toys yourself, by actively playing with your cat. Some cats respond better to a person playing with them, because it's more exciting to them. Try to play with your cat at least once a day for 15 minutes. And have lively toys available for the other times.

Fresh Air is Necessary

Cats do not like stale air any more than you do. Fresh air is refreshing to them as well as healthy for them. All air-breathing creatures feel better physically when they get fresh air because it has more pure oxygen in it. So make sure the air in your home is fresh.

The best way to do this is to keep at least one window in your home open as much, and as often, as possible. Cats really enjoy sitting on a window sill while taking in the sights, sounds, and scents of the outdoors.

In the winter, solariums are a nice alternative to an open window. They are a clear enclosure that protrudes from the window, allowing your cat to sit "outside" without the window being open.

Cats Need Their Space

Cats are independent creatures. But indoor cats do not have as much independence, because they have less space to roam. Therefore, it is important to allow your cat to "get away" within your home.

To do this, take notice of where your cat likes to go for privacy and make sure not to "invade" these places with objects. You can also create places for your cat to retreat to, by making a little spot in the corner of a closet or room. You can put a small towel or blanket in it, and maybe some toys, if that is something your cat would like.

Having a "cat tree" or "cat condo" in your home will give your cat their own area, to climb and hide in, that they can call their own. You can create your own "cat tree" by clearing off, and keeping clear, a spot on a table or a certain chair that your cat can jump up on.

Your Cat will Appreciate it

It is important to give your cat what it needs, because they are living creatures and dependent on you. Playing, fresh air, and freedom are equally important needs that will take some creativity to provide for your indoor cat. But it can be done and, especially if it's maintained, your cat will thank you. Your special animal friend is definitely worth the effort.

Sources

National Geographic -
http://www.animals.nationalgeographic.com/animals/mammals/domestic-cat

Key Elements of a Happy Marriage

No two marriages are the same, and each situation a married couple encounters requires specialized care and attention. Friends and family can offer advice, but really the situation is unique because both people in the marriage are unique, and ultimately, they will make decisions that are best for their marriage. With that said, there are certain elements for happy marriages that are universal for married couples. If these elements are integrated, the marriage will be healthier and happier.

Open Communication

A husband and wife cannot read each other's mind. That is why open communication helps relationships run smoother. In a marriage, effective communication is essential for the couple to get along. Regardless of how many years they've been together, spouses cannot know each other's every need. Oftentimes, wives will hint at what they want because they don't want to state their needs directly. But, husbands are not always good at understanding or recognizing hints. So it is important for a married couple to communicate assertively and honestly. It is also important for couples to outgrow their shyness (if they tend to be shy in public) in order to communicate well with each other. Sharing thoughts, goals, activities, and desires increases the connection between a husband and wife.

Compromises

In all marriages, compromise allows the couple to get along. No two people have the same beliefs, so spouses should make compromises to maintain fairness. A compromise benefits both spouses in a marriage and it will avoid anyone having hurt feelings. A compromise is also the best way to end disagreements quickly. Disagreements do not mean that only one person is wrong; rather, disagreements mean conflicting opinions. It is very difficult for a person to convince someone else to change his or her perspective in order to completely agree with the person, because people rarely change, except out of personal choice. So, compromises provide a resolution and allow the couple to easily move on with their lives.

Individual Interests and Friends

A married couple consists of two individuals, of course. Yes, they are united by vows; but they should also remain involved in activities that interest them. Some of their interests will differ, and they should still pursue those separate interests occasionally. Variety of interests brings spontaneity and excitement into a marriage. It gives a couple things to talk about. It also helps the couple get along better, because their time apart will make them feel grateful they are united. It is important for spouses to maintain their individuality when they get married in order to maintain their personalities.

Loving Each Other's Personality

Married couples that love each other's personality, will have long-lasting marriages. They will have less fights; they will enjoy spending time together; and they will be grateful for being united. They will stay together for many years, because they will not want to be with anyone else. They will be happy with their spouse for as long as they are in love. It is very easy for a couple to be happy and faithful if they are in love.

Having a Long-Lasting Marriage

Marriages take constant work. They involve two people that typically spend a lot of time together and need to make decisions, deal with finances, as well as other responsibilities. In fact, marriages are sometimes stressful. However, the key elements to a happy marriage will help a couple get along, love each other, and live a long, happy life together.

Tips for Better Communication with your Spouse

Effective communication is very important in a marriage. However, some couples do not put in effort to improve their communication. Developing or maintaining effective communication should be a goal in all marriages. There is a way for spouses to improve their exchanges. The following steps will lead to improved communication between spouses.

1. Initiate a Discussion

First, the couple needs to bring up the topic of communication. Someone must initiate the discussion, so one spouse can do so by using an email or note, especially if the other spouse is unaware of their wishes. A note or email might also avoid an argument, if a communication issue they have is frequent arguing.

The email or note should say that the spouse wants to get together soon to talk about communication and how they can improve their communication skills as a couple. The spouse should also write that he or she cares very much about his or her spouse and the union they share, or something similar. The message should also suggest a certain time to meet for the discussion.

2. Set the Scene

On the day and time they decided to have the discussion on communication, the spouses should sit down together and begin by talking about their strengths with communication and the positives in their marriage. This will set the scene for a more civil discussion about improvements they need to make. They should notice and emphasize the closeness forming between them from the positive talk, and possibly feeling friendly and being on the same "side" in the discussion.

3. The Discussion

Once compatibility and peacefulness is established, the spouses can begin discussing how they think they can improve communication between them. Each spouse can share thoughts about what they personally need to improve upon. It is important to try to remain civil and calm, and not interrupt each other. Examples of communication topics that can be discussed are: communicating more often, getting along better, being more "open," improving the quality of discussions about important issues in their marriage, being kinder when communicating, sharing about themselves equally, and so on.

Goals - such as being friends rather than enemies - should be established, as well as a plan - series of steps - on how to achieve the goals. It is best for each spouse to have personal goals, and also to have general goals as a couple.

4. Carry out the Plan and Achieve the Goals

The spouses should give equal effort to follow through with the plan to improve their communication skills. They should work on personal goals individually, and also help each other to reach the personal - and general - goals. It is a good idea to occasionally remind each other of their communication discussion and general goals when one, or both, of them gets off track. If both happen to get lenient with their efforts and lose sight of their goals, or if one of them gives up on reaching his or her goals, they should repeat all the steps above until both spouses have improved their communication skills to an acceptable level for a substantial amount of time. Follow up with future discussions as needed.

Summary

The purpose of the steps is for the spouses to have a civil discussion about communication when the need arises, give equal effort to improve their communication skills individually and as a couple, and follow up when either of them gets derailed from their plan to reach their goals.

Effective communication is possible when spouses give equal effort to communicate well with each other and to have calm and mature discussions when their communication skills need improvement. Following the steps above will improve communication between spouses and will lead to long-lasting marriages.

Ways to Show Appreciation for your Husband

Appreciation between spouses is important in a marriage. It is a way to show they care about each other and it strengthens the marriage. A wife can show her husband appreciation by being affectionate, reciprocating what he does, being supportive, and not try to change him. They are all equally effective ways for her to show appreciation for the man she loves.

Be Affectionate

A wife being affectionate towards her husband is a caring way to show her appreciation for him. This can be subtle or obvious, and best if both. Husbands tend to notice obvious affection more easily. A wife can show affection by cuddling up to her husband while they watch television. She can also massage his shoulders after a stressful day or give him a hug just because she loves him. He will appreciate his wife's affection and will likely show it back.

Reciprocate his Actions

A great way for a wife to show appreciation for what her husband does, is to do the same for him. For example, if he often holds the door open for her when they enter buildings, she can take the initiative to hold the door open for him sometimes. Another example is, when he does chores around the house, she can join in and do chores at the same time to make the task easier for her husband. If he cooks dinner, buys her flowers, or takes care of the kids, she can show appreciation for him by returning the favors.

Be Supportive

Husbands often feel like they need to take care of everything and be strong, but they need support sometimes too. There are various ways a wife can be supportive of her husband. She can listen to his concerns during a tough time, help out with the finances, and offer her most thoughtful advice when he has a problem he would like to resolve. He will likely notice her efforts, and even though he may not admit it, he will be glad for the help. Being supportive of her husband when he needs it, shows she understands and appreciates all he does for their marriage.

Accept him

An excellent way for a wife to show appreciation for her husband, is by loving and accepting him as he is. By showing her approval of his personality and actions - through smiling, eye contact, and gestures - he will see her appreciation for him. Being less critical of him and not trying to change him, is a great way to show her appreciation. Accepting him for who he is leads to more loving moments.

Your Appreciation will be Appreciated

A well-rounded manner for a wife to show appreciation for her husband involves: being affectionate, reciprocating his actions, being supportive, and accepting him. Her actions can be emotional, mental, or financial in nature. Above all, any way that a wife can show appreciation for her husband will be appreciated back.

CHAPTER 4

FINANCIAL PLANNING, FRUGAL LIVING, AND MONEY

Bankruptcy and Budgeting: How to Start Over

Starting over after a bankruptcy can be challenging. For one, you may not get approved for credit right away. And it also takes effort and skill to avoid falling into debt again. Therefore, you must have a plan on how to handle your finances now that you have a fresh start. There are several things you can do:

1. Compute your Monthly Budget

The most basic, but most important, way to recover after a bankruptcy is to come up with, or amend, your budget. Obviously, some changes need to be made to your budget in order to avoid falling back into debt. To create a monthly budget chart, total all of your income sources and all of your expenses. Figure in yearly expenses as well. Include everything - even the most minor details. Round up on expenses and round down on income to make sure all of your expenses will be covered. Be realistic with what you put in your budget chart.

2. Follow your Budget

People are typically sensible about their finances when they initially create a budget chart. But in order to continue with the sensibility, and follow through, you should follow the chart exactly as it's laid out. If you find that your budget is not working right for you, change the chart. But always make sure you follow your chart so you don't get off track.

3. Limit Credit Card Use

Until you know if your budget is effective, avoid using credit cards. In fact, it is good to live without credit cards for the first year. They are little loans, and therefore, can be troublesome, so avoiding them for a while is wise. First make sure you can live off your income and follow your budget month to month. Then, if you wish, slowly introduce credit cards back into your life. If you use a credit card to make a purchase, use it only in emergencies or if you have the cash in your account to cover the charges.

4. Accrue a Savings Account

Deposit some money into a savings account each month. This will help you in two ways:

1. The money can come in handy for unexpected expenses.
2. It gets you out of the habit of living paycheck to paycheck.

In other words, it will help you look into the future and plan for it. Underestimating expenses is what gets many people stuck in high-debt situations. So by doing the opposite - making sure money is left over after expenses are covered - you are sure to be successful with budgeting your finances.

5. Apply for Credit

Years down the road, when you have a handle on your budget and finances, you may want to try applying for credit in order to reestablish your credit rating. This could be any type of credit that you think you can handle. It is not necessary to avoid credit for the rest of your life because you've had a bankruptcy; rather, the point is to relearn how to manage your finances and credit. When requesting credit, be realistic, and avoid situations that may be problematic for you.

Now that you've mastered your budget, developed a savings account, and rebuilt your credit, you are well on your way to a satisfactory credit rating and financial situation. The most important thing to remember is, in order to avoid mistakes, you must learn from past experiences and have a plan for the future.

Basics of Creating a Household Budget

Every household should have a household budget. That is because it is necessary to know if you can afford your bills with your income. It is also helpful to know your monthly income and expenses ahead of time. Creating a household budget can be as simple or elaborate as you want. Below are the steps to creating a basic household budget.

1. Compile a List of Your Household Expenses

Take a blank piece of paper and list all your expenses. If you have a lot of expenses (more than ten) you can group them, such as: utilities, credit cards, healthcare, etc. and put subcategories, such as: heat, electricity, and phone (utilities). Don't forget to include expenses that are paid for less often than once a month.

2. Compute Monthly Expense Amounts

Next to each expense in the list, put the monthly cost, and round up to the nearest 5 or 10. For example, a regular monthly bill for $53.46 would be listed as $55. Rounding will keep your numbers neater when they're in the computer. If the expense is yearly, such as house tax, divide the highest amount it would cost by 12. If the expense is several times a year, divide the amount by how often it is paid; for example, for a life insurance expense that is paid once every three months, divide the bill by three to give you the monthly amount. On the other hand, if it's a weekly expense, such as groceries, multiply the highest amount you pay in a week by 4.3 (average number of weeks in a month). A calculator will be of great help to you.

3. Compile a List of Household Income Types and Amounts

Take another piece of paper and write down all of your household income. List the types of income and the monthly amounts. Compute monthly amounts the same as you did with expenses; but instead use the minimum amount and round down. Many people get into trouble financially because they overestimate their income and underestimate their bills. This system avoids that.

4. Finish Sketching Your Household Budget

Expenses and income are the most important parts of a monthly budget. However, you can add other helpful sections, such as: responsibility (the person responsible for the expense), goals, savings, and investments. Write the title and section headings, and draw the columns and rows, on all your charts.

5. Create a Spreadsheet in Microsoft Excel (or similar software)

Open Microsoft Excel. Give your document a name, such as "family budget," and save it in "documents" or another folder that you'll easily be able to locate. At the bottom of the Excel spreadsheet are tabs that are labeled sheet 1, sheet 2, and sheet 3. You can change these names to expenses, income, and savings, as well as add more sheets, depending on how many different charts you want. Put your title across the top of the chart and fill in your data as you have already drawn out. At the bottom of the columns with figures, put a total. If you are skilled with Excel formulas (great!), you can use them to make updating the household budget easier. But if you don't know formulas, that's okay; you can still click the "autosum" button to total your figures at the bottom.

6. Put the Finishing Touches on Your Household Budget

You may also format the chart by making the headings bold so they will stand out better to you, and make the columns and rows wide enough so that all the information is visible. After you are all done, as well as periodically throughout the process, save your work. You can print your household budget or just save it on the computer for reference.

7. Analyze the Details of Your Budget

Hopefully you will find that your income is higher than your expenses. If so, great! The savings sheet will be of great help to you with budgeting your extra income. If you find your income does not cover all your expenses, it's good that you now know and you can see what needs to be done to mend it. You may decide to cut back on certain expenses or seek out more income. One important thing to keep in mind, is that you must set aside money for expenses that are due less often than once a month. It is easy to forget those less-frequent expenses, and it can hurt your finances if they are not taken into account each month.

Now that your household budget is finalized, you only need to update the chart as information changes. You are now more organized and efficient about your household finances. A thriving household is well-worth the time spent creating a household budget.

Frugal Living: Developing a Kitchen Pantry Using Grocery Sales Cycles and Coupons

Being frugal takes practice. Some people have lived with a tight budget their entire life. Other people have experienced economic hardships that hit unexpectedly. Either way, the skills of frugal living must be learned and developed. Living inexpensively is easy to learn, and it provides a lifetime of significant savings.

The grocery store is where money goes fast for many households. You have to eat, so slight price increases are usually overlooked. However, there are incredible savings available to you there in the form of weekly sales and coupons. It is wise to learn the best way to use these tools in order to save yourself the most money.

Buy What is Cheapest

When grocery shopping on a limited budget, the goal is to spend as little as possible. That means you will usually buy the store brand items (especially if they are on sale), even if a name brand item is on sale. Store brand items taste very similar to name brand items and they are adequate if saving money is important to you. On the other hand, if the cost of a name brand item on sale is less than the store brand, pick it up.

Stock up on Sale Items

Stock up on your favorite items and items that don't get marked down often (such as milk) when they go on sale. (Stocking up simply means buying more than one shopping cycle's worth of the item; so if you usually shop once a week - buying more than what you would

107

consume of the item in a week is stocking up.) Also stock up on items you use that are marked down to clearance, because it is probably the cheapest they'll ever get.

Take the Time to Clip Coupons

Coupons are very worthwhile. Start spending time looking through newspapers, magazines, weekly inserts, and certain websites. Clip as many coupons as possible that will be useful. To determine "useful" - imagine having the item in your pantry or refrigerator. Will you use the item in a reasonable amount of time? If not, don't clip it. It is paper and time that will be wasted, so it's likely not worth it. There will be plenty of other opportunities to save.

No Coupon or Sale is Worth it if You Won't Use the Item

Use a coupon on an item only if it will benefit you. Ask yourself if you are going to use the entire item and if the coupon will make the item cheaper than the store brand item. The bottom-line: only use a coupon, or buy something on sale, if it is an item you regularly use or would like to use for a new recipe or a different meal.

More Variety and Better Nutrition

Because sales change weekly and new coupons come out daily, your kitchen pantry will have a wide variety of foods in it, which means a tastier and more nutritious diet. This is because eating an array of foods will keep your food choices interesting, as well as provide well-balanced nutrition.

Additional Savings and Tips

The best choice you can make when shopping at the grocery store, is to use a coupon on a sale or clearance item. Typically that is the biggest savings you can get on one item. Some grocery stores double the coupons, so claim those opportunities as they occur. It is best to find a grocery store you like that is most beneficial to your budget. However, shopping at more than one grocery store will save you even more money, because every store has different items and sales. That means you will have an even larger variety of foods in your pantry and a lot more savings. Just make sure the additional traveling is worthwhile.

The best part about shopping frugally at the grocery store, besides saving a lot of money, is that you are more likely to try out new foods, because the varying sales and coupons encourage it. So be creative, spontaneous, and a little bold by seeking out coupons, rummaging for the cheapest items, and shopping around. The savings will make you very glad you did!

How Financial Planning Makes a Difference

Financial planning can keep you from being homeless. Financial planning allows you to save and invest in your future. Financial planning lowers stress. There are many reasons why financial planning is good to do. In fact, everyone should have some idea, budget, or plan when they have income and bills to pay. The rewards of financial planning are well worth it.

Maintain a Budget

To begin a financial plan, start by creating a household budget chart on the computer. At bare minimum, a budget will keep record of income and expenses. How are you supposed to buy something, or pay for anything, if you don't know if you can afford it? Don't say 'charge it on a credit card' because lingering debt only makes a struggling financial situation worse. That is why it is important to maintain a record of your budget that will let you know how much you can afford to spend without going into debt. Going into debt is truthfully the first step in the direction of filing for bankruptcy or becoming homeless.

Keep an Active Savings Account

So, you stick to your budget and can get by every month with your current income and no credit card debt? That's great. However, life 'happens' and changes occur. You need to be prepared for emergencies. If you didn't get paid one month, how would you cover your rent and food expenses? That is the reason why it is good to save money. In fact, it is best to save every month and every chance you get. The amount you can save is relative and isn't as important as the act of not spending all the week's or month's income. That takes skill and perseverance. The important part is getting in the habit of saving money from every pay. In other words, save money when you have it for the times when you won't. For example, $100 in your savings account will really come in handy one week when you don't have grocery money.

Invest in Retirement and the Future

In addition to having a savings account for emergencies, it is important to invest in your retirement. Just think about, when you can no longer work and become retired, if you don't have a retirement fund, you will only receive Social Security benefits, which is not generous income to say the least. So ask yourself: could you realistically survive on only Social Security for income? The answer is likely probably not or barely. While you are able to set aside money, it is a good idea to put some of it towards retirement. You will be glad you did.

When considering financial planning, think beyond today, this week, or this month. Think a year ahead and decades ahead even. If you do not think of your future, you may find yourself in a tight financial situation with nowhere to go. By then it is too late to do anything. So, do something now. No matter how little money you have, you can find a small amount to set aside regularly for the future. It will make all the difference in the world.

How to Use Credit Cards Wisely

In truth, credit cards are a bad habit for many people. Some individuals find themselves in debts that they can't readily or always get out of. There are numerous companies nowadays offering credit services to help people manage their debts. And there is the dreaded bankruptcy that is used as a last resort, but at least is a workable solution. So, why are credit cards so difficult to manage?

It has to do with the fact that credit cards are a miniature loan with a monthly bill. It is easy for someone to forget what and how much they buy throughout the month, either mistakenly or intentionally. Purchases add up quickly and pretty soon they have overspent their budget. Then when they receive the bill, they are unable to pay off the entire balance. Therefore, it carries over to the next month's bill, plus additional fees and surcharges. It is difficult to catch up by under-spending the next month, so typically the balance forward grows larger.

It is important to realize exactly how credit cards work for many people in order to avoid making similar mistakes. Naturally, people like to shop for new things, because it is rewarding to treat oneself. But, it is important to keep in mind that a budget is generally limited, so if it is exceeded there will be financial trouble.

The wisest way to use credit cards, firstly, is not to have too many. Owning one or two credit cards is plenty. In some instances only credit cards are accepted as a payment form, such as when renting a car or booking a plane; therefore a credit card is good to have. Just remember that the more credit cards a person has, the more difficult it is to keep track of the balances.

The best way to handle credit cards is first to figure out monthly expenditures. Count everything you spend money on and don't leave anything out, because every dollar counts. Don't forget about expenses that aren't always monthly, such as hair appointments and doctor visits. For those you add up the total cost for one year and divide by twelve, to make it a monthly expense amount.

If you don't know exactly how much you spend on something, because it varies, then round up on an estimate or choose the highest possible price it could be. Finally, add up all your household income and subtract your total expenses. Whatever amount is left over is the most you can charge on your credit card each month. And no matter what, do not overcharge that amount. Ultimately, if you can't afford it, you shouldn't have it.

By staying within your credit card budget you will be able to pay off the balance each month. That means – as long as you make the payments on time – you will not lose anything to penalty charges. Plus, if you have some type of cash back reward program with your credit card company, then you will actually gain money from owning a credit card.

Making timely payments is just as important as paying off the balance each month. To do so, figure out your income schedule one month in advance to determine which pay period you will need to make the credit card payment from. That way, you will be able to afford the payment and have it received prior to the due date. Mail your check or money order one week before the due date, so that you won't have to worry about it getting there on time. One week is adequate time, even considering weekends and holidays. If you can afford to mail it sooner, then by all means do so.

There were five main aspects of how to use credit cards wisely that were covered in this article:

1. Think about how to avoid credit card pitfalls.
2. Figure out your monthly budget.
3. Don't charge more than your leftover money.
4. Determine what pay period you will use to make the payment.
5. Mail the payment one week in advance.

If you follow through with these five details, you will surely be an expert credit card user.

Should you Lease or Buy Your Next Car?

To buy or lease a car is an important choice to make and should be made wisely. Luckily, if the determining factors are weighed evenly, it is fairly easy to arrive at the best choice. The factors to consider are your finances, needs, and future. There are several questions you should ask yourself before buying or leasing a car.

How Much Driving Will You Be Doing?

If you travel often, take a lot of road trips, and have a long commute between home and work, or if you think you will be putting a lot of mileage on the car, buying a car may be wise. You should keep in mind that most lease terms only allow for mileage 15,000 miles a year or less. Any mileage over the set limit will receive high fees when the vehicle is returned. So, if you drive more than 15,000 miles a year, or think you will be, leasing is not a good option.

Do You Have Kids?

Please note that you must return a leased car and there are limits on the amount of 'wear and tear' that is acceptable, so you could accrue financial penalties if you cause too much internal or external damage. Because kids in general tend to be less careful and make more messes than most adults, you might want to consider additional insurance coverage in the lease terms. Or if you think damages could occur from using the car, that are more than normal due to kids or pets, you may want to buy a car because then you won't have to worry about any additional charges.

Are You Responsible?

If you take very good care of your belongings, keep things clean, and are conscientious about your actions, leasing would be a fine option for you. However, if you tend to lose things easily, are more casual or neglecting with your life and possessions, and are not careful to avoid mistakes, leasing could become a problematic situation, because car damages could occur that you might not be able to afford.

How Much Can You Afford?

When considering this question, think about the present as well as the future. For instance, if you can afford to make higher payments now and you wish to have no payments in the future - out of preference or because you are uncertain about your financial situation in the future - then buying a car may be the better choice. On the other hand, if you are on a limited income and budget that doesn't change much, and you can't afford much of a monthly payment, leasing is your best bet.

Those are the main questions to ask yourself, and really think about, before buying or leasing a car. Make sure you are honest with yourself, think about the future, and especially, consider your income and financial situation. The goal is to avoid getting into a financial predicament, and to instead make the wisest decision for you and your household.

Tips on How to be Happy When You are Poor

Being poor does not mean that you have to be unhappy. In fact, money does not create true, inner happiness. Having money may reduce stress because money is required to survive in the world. But it is very possible to be happy when you are poor, and there are lots of opportunities to enjoy life when you don't have much money to spend. The following are things you can do to enjoy life and be happy when you are poor.

Have a Clean Living Space

Staying inside and doing housework does not cost much money - just the cost of cleaning supplies. Taking care of your inside environment by picking up, organizing, and straightening your belongings, as well as doing housework and cleaning, will provide feelings of contentment and satisfaction from the natural reward of productivity, achievement, and having a pleasant looking - and smelling - living space. Cleaning is good for the soul and body. You will get exercise from the activity, and you will feel pleased with yourself for accomplishing challenging tasks.

Experience Natural Outdoor Exercise

Exercising does not have to cost money. Forget about gym memberships and expensive exercise equipment. Instead, go for a fast-paced walk for as long as you can. Go to a park and participate in the activities they have; for instance, some parks have running tracks, tennis courts, or walking paths. Go hiking on trails in the woods or on a mountain. Hiking simply means walking on a surface that is not flat, so any hill would suffice. Don't forget to bring lots of water to drink. You can make the activity last longer by packing a lunch, blanket, and book for a relaxing break when you need it. You will feel great to get outside in the fresh air and move your body. The endorphins released during exercise will make you feel pleasant, content, and happy.

Do Recreational Activities and Hobbies

Reading, writing, drawing, cooking, yoga, and music, are all great ways to feel good without spending much money. All it takes is paper and a pen to write and draw for hours. You can borrow books from a library to read and the supply of books is endless. Cooking is cheaper than buying packaged meals and it tastes better. You can learn to cook or try out new recipes. You must eat, so why not have fun, by being creative, with it? You can read a book about yoga and then practice the moves. You can also make up your own stretches and poses once you understand the theory of yoga. There are plenty of ways to entertain yourself and have fun inexpensively.

Make Self-Care and Relaxation Special

Light a few candles, turn on some soft music, and soak in the tub. It will instantly start to relax you and decrease your stress from the day. Give yourself a manicure and pedicure by trimming your nails and cuticles, and then put lotion on your hands and feet. Turn off the lights and sit on something comfortable that supports your back; once situated, close your eyes, focus on your deep breaths, observe how your mind clears, and let stress release from your body; do this for 15-20 minutes to feel peaceful, grateful, and content. Making self-care special will make you feel important and happy.

Go Out and Have Fun Without Spending Much

If you have two dollars you can go to a cafe, purchase a drink, and stay there as long as you want while listening to karaoke singers, a musician, or a band; socializing and making new friends; or just observing the different people and enjoying the ambiance. If you have five dollars, you can see a matinee and bring your own snacks and drinks to enjoy. If you enjoy window shopping and it doesn't tempt you to buy, you can go walking at a mall with a friend, and take silly pictures in the photo booth or enjoy a beverage and conversation in the food court.

As you can see, life can be very enjoyable and not require much money. Happiness can be experienced while enjoying what you have and making the best of it. Good company, and situations that are made special, is what makes life enjoyable and makes you feel happy. Happiness is an internal feeling that is not affected by how much money is spent, but instead, by your view of life and yourself. Any moment can be made into a happy one, regardless of the amount of money you have.

What—Besides Wealth—Are Measures of Prosperity?

Prosperity originates from professional, educational, and personal goals. It indirectly asks people to improve upon themselves, and as a result, self-awareness is enhanced. Advancing in any way, or initiating positive change, is prosperity. Educational, professional, and personal are different types of prosperity, and they are equally important.

Educational Prosperity

Prosperity is about far more than obtaining riches and status, for there are other types of treasures in the world. For example, the feeling you get from gaining knowledge is highly rewarding.

Increased knowledge of the world is the most wholesome type of prosperity. Continually learning, sharing, and listening—to have an active mind, improve insight, and increase wisdom—is a fulfilling way to live.

It is important for prosperous people to always consider themselves students. If you are alive, you are a student, and the world is your teacher. Life is about learning, and the knowledge gained should be constructively applied to helping the future. That is the way the human race develops, evolves, and survives.

Professional Prosperity

Professional prosperity does not necessarily mean an increase in salary. It can also represent an increase in confidence and success at work, whatever and wherever that may be. When an employee is successful at work, they usually become self-assured about their professional abilities; consequently, their supervisors notice and that leads to professional advancement. The confidence-success cycle is continuous.

In addition, when a prolific employee shows interest in learning new skills, and they have already mastered their present duties, they may be rewarded with a higher position or new responsibilities. That is a professional compliment to an employee, and it is a gratifying transition and accomplishment for employees who wish to progress and prosper.

Professional prosperity begins with a single thought of wanting to improve, create, change, or advance at work. The feelings typically experienced are: drive, determination, ambition, and/or motivation. The thoughts in their mind may be an innovative idea that they want to take action on.

Negative life events can eventually lead to professional prosperity. For instance, losing a job often motivates people to take action on their future, possibly by furthering their education and searching for a better job.

Personal Prosperity

Prosperity is also about fulfilling personal goals. The best way to succeed at this is for the person to write down a list of smaller goals that will keep them on the desired path. Every time a smaller goal is met, the desire to accomplish more is gained.

Personal prosperity is not a grand, final event, but is rather the accomplishment of small goals along the path of life. There is always the ability to prosper. In fact, prosperity's boundless limits makes for endless success.

***

Prosperity requires action. Motivation gives people the direction they need to accomplish. Accomplishments, whether educational, professional, or personal, are the most motivating events in the world. With plenty of opportunities to accomplish, there is always the ability to prosper.

CHAPTER 5

FOOD, HOLIDAYS, AND HOME

Bathroom Clutter Control Tips

Bathroom clutter is a problem for many households. It is especially troublesome for large families who have kids. However, it is possible to have a tidy bathroom. Using the following three methods will lessen and control the amount of clutter in your bathroom.

Hang up Numerous Hooks

Wet towels are everywhere and there are not enough towel racks to hang them all. Sound familiar? One helpful tip is to take down the racks and install some hooks on the walls to use instead. A towel rack - a horizontal bar screwed into the wall that holds one bath towel - takes up to five times more wall space than one hook. Therefore, installing five hooks in the place of one rack, will provide places for four extra wet towels to hang and dry. Using hooks instead of racks will make the bathroom look neater, because there will be places to hang all the towels.

Install a Cabinet Over the Toilet

Often, in bathrooms the wall space above the toilet is bare, because it is an odd place to put something. A towel rack or artwork are typically the only things that are put in that space, which is not very useful when you are trying to make best use out of your space. However, there are cabinets that are portable and stand above the toilet or screw into the wall. These are relatively inexpensive, can store a significant amount, and make the bathroom neater. Some of these fixtures are shelves, some are cabinets, and some are a combination of both. You can store anything in them - from extra towels, to paper products, to beauty supplies. If you prefer, you can even make your own over-the-toilet cabinet fixture yourself.

Tidy up Once a Week

It is easy for the bathroom to get cluttered if it's not maintained properly. It is recommended to look through, organize, and straighten up once a week. Dispose of empty containers, remove dirty towels, throw out - or store in other locations - items you don't use often, refold clean towels to look neater, and empty the trash. By organizing your bathroom once a week, it will maintain its neat state.

A Few Changes and a Little Effort Means Less Stress

It is impossible to have a completely clutter-free bathroom. The clutter just "happens" from regular use. But if there are hooks for all the wet towels, a cabinet for storage, and a quick tidying job done once a week, the bathroom will be much less cluttered and more productive and efficient. Because the bathroom is less cluttered, you will be less stressed, and that makes the small amount of effort it takes well worth it.

Best Ways to Thaw Frozen Meat

Freezing is a good way to preserve meat for extended periods of time. When it is time to take a serving of meat down from the freezer, there are three different ways to best thaw it: in the refrigerator, in cold water, and in the microwave. The best method is determined by how soon until the thawed meat needs to be cooked.

In the Refrigerator

Frozen meat takes twenty-four hours to thaw in the refrigerator. Large items take twenty-four hours for every five pounds (National Center for Home Food Preservation). Therefore, thawing meat in the refrigerator is best if you have at least a whole day before the meat needs to be cooked. Make sure to put a plate under the package of meat to catch drippings as it thaws. Make sure to turn the package of meat over a few times to thaw it evenly on all sides. Meat thawed slowly and evenly will cook better. Once thawed, the meat should be cooked within a day or two to avoid bacteria growth. You can also re-freeze meat that was thawed in the refrigerator, but it may compromise the quality (The Cook's Thesaurus).

In Cold Water

To speed up the thawing process, you can put the meat in cold water. Keep in mind, this method should only be used if the meat will thaw in less than two hours (National Center for Home Food Preservation). Put the package of frozen meat in a sealed plastic bag and run cold water over it. Make sure to turn the package occasionally to thaw it evenly. Or you can put the bag of meat in cold water in the sink; but remember to replace the water with fresh cold water every half-hour to keep the meat cool in order to prevent bacteria growth. The more water used, and the more the water moves, the quicker the meat will thaw. The meat should be cooked immediately after it is thawed in cold water (The Cook's Thesaurus).

In the Microwave

For last-minute meals -- situations when you don't have much time to thaw the meat -- you can use a microwave. However, this should be done with extreme caution to avoid over-cooking the meat. The goal is to simply thaw it - making it no longer frozen - but not warmed or cooked. The best way to do this is to use the defrost button or use a low power level.

If using the defrost button, you will need to enter the weight of the meat and press "start." The microwave will beep two or more times during the defrosting process, in which you should open the microwave door and turn the meat package over; this is to defrost evenly. You should not rely on the defrost setting to decide when the meat is done thawing, because the settings may not be accurate and there are many variables and factors involved, such as the temperature the meat was frozen at, and the condition and wattage of the microwave. Touch the meat package occasionally and try to feel for the center. If it still feels cold, it is not defrosted yet. When the center of the meat package is at a temperature that's just slightly cool to the touch, it is correctly defrosted and should be cooked right away.

Thawing frozen meat is a process. But, it must be done, and with a little practice you will learn how to do it properly. The more gradual you let meat thaw, the more evenly it will cook. So if you can, try to plan your meals involving meat ahead of time. But if you cannot, the options above are available to you.

Sources

National Center for Home Preservation -
www.nchfp.uga.edu/how/freeze/thawing.html

The Cook's Thesaurus -
www.sonic.net/~alden/Defrost.html

How to Lower Energy Costs From Home Appliance Use

Energy costs are a common concern. With the increase in electricity rates, people are looking for ways to conserve energy. Since home appliances often consume a lot of energy, they should be monitored to save money. This article will review how to tend to the three most energy-consuming appliances so that you can save money.

Computers

Computers require a lot of electricity to run. Computer use is increasing as more people purchase home computers and also use them more often. Plus, there is an increasing number of people that work from home and spend a good deal of time on the computer. The best way to conserve computer energy is to put the computer in "sleep mode" when using it intermittently, and shut it down completely when not using it. Do not leave your computer running all the time just because you use it often. We all sleep and we all go out to run errands. So turn your computer off during those times.

Lights

Many people leave lights on unnecessarily. If you are not spending much time in a room, there is no need to have a light on in it. Do not leave lights on for convenience. It is best have only one or two lights left on at a time. Turning on a light when you enter a room and turning it off when you leave is the proper thing to do. Make it replace your old habit of leaving too many lights on. If you do, you will end up conserving energy and save money.

There are also energy-efficient light bulbs that use less electricity. Yes, these are more expensive than old-fashioned light bulbs, but you will save money in the long run.

Televisions

Televisions are used often in households and require a lot of electricity when they are on. This is an issue when you are trying to lower energy costs. However, there are ways to resolve it. If your household makes an effort to watch TV together, the TV will be on less often. To do this, pick the best times for everyone to gather and watch TV where it is on only if at least two people are watching it. And keep the TV turned off the rest of the day.

Appliances that use electricity are popular, because they are convenient. It is easy to get complacent with appliances and leave them running when not in use. However, to save energy costs, it is important to keep an eye on your appliance use. The planet will thank you too.

How to Reorganize a Messy File Cabinet

It is important to stay organized, both at home and at work. A file cabinet is helpful with doing so, but only if it's neat and systematic. Occasionally, file cabinets get cluttered and disorganized. That is when it's time to reorganize them so that they will once again work effectively and efficiently. There are several steps involved with reorganizing a messy file cabinet.

Step 1

Starting at the front of the file cabinet, remove all the paperwork from the first file. As you go through it, make two piles: one for the majority of the paperwork that is related, and one for miscellaneous, misfiled paperwork. Take the first pile (related paperwork) and group documents of the same type together in date order, from newest (in the front) to oldest, and attach a paperclip or binder clip. Order these clipped documents from most important, or most needed, to least needed, from the front of the file to the back. This will help you find paperwork more quickly. Repeat this process for every file in the file cabinet.

Step 2

As you sort through the paperwork, determine how far back in time you need to keep paperwork for. Likely, you will need to look up recent paperwork most often, so it is best to have that readily available and separate from the older documents. You may find that you will have different date guidelines depending on the type of paperwork. For instance, tax returns are done yearly and you will want to save several years of supporting documents; versus shopping receipts, which occur more often and are not as crucial to save, especially the older they get. Set aside the oldest paperwork to be dealt with later.

Step 3

Now that you have the majority of your paperwork grouped into the files, it is time to keep, revise, or create the labels for each folder. Glance at the contents of each folder and decide if the current label on the folder is an accurate description for the contents. If it is, then just leave it. If it is not, then revise the label or create a new one. Use only 1 to 2 words on each label and write clearly and neatly. Make sure every folder with contents in it has a corresponding label. Then, arrange the folders alphabetically by the first word on each label.

Step 4

Pick up the pile of miscellaneous paperwork that was set aside from each file. For each paper, consider the date and importance of it and decide if it should be filed in one of the folders, kept separate (if old), or disposed of (if not needed). If you choose to file it, do so neatly and according to the system already established. Paperwork that you decide to keep separate can be filed in a folder labeled "old" and put in the back of the file cabinet or filed in a small, separate file cabinet using the same system of organization as the main cabinet. Which method you choose depends on the quantity of leftover paperwork (a large quantity may need to be organized in a separate location, but a small quantity could easily be put in a single file).

If you followed the steps and suggestions above, your file cabinet is now a neat and organized system that will be more efficient and effective for you to be organized and on top of your paperwork. Maintain the neatness of your file cabinet by repeating the outlined steps every six months. You will find paperwork you need more easily and will likely feel relief from being organized.

Ideas for a Romantic Christmas Dinner for Two

Christmas is a joyful time of year that is usually spent with family, friends, and loved ones. It is a chance to get together, share memories, and enjoy giving. Christmas can also be thought of as a romantic holiday for new couples and for couples who have been together for half-a-lifetime. Christmas dinner is very important for couples who wish to spend the holiday together. There are ways to make Christmas dinnertime romantic.

Decorate Festively

First, you should decorate. Try using silver and gold accents to add a romantic touch. Make the task of decorating a combined effort. Embellish the dining room, or the entire home, with ornaments, pictures, cards, crafts, wreaths, and other decorations that hold a special meaning for you two as a couple. You can also spend time helping each other decorate the Christmas tree. Then, dim the lights, sit back in each other's arms, and admire all the decorating you have done together.

Plan the Dinner

Every important dinner needs a plan. What will you make? How much? What will you use for place settings? The two of you can discuss what you want for dinner and how you want the dinner to go, and then make a final decision based on the most agreed upon ideas. Print out the recipes you decide on, and choose which tasks you will each take care of. You may also want to decide how many plates and bowls you will need, and if you want to have a dessert.

Cook Together

Now that there is a dinner plan, you can begin on the task of preparing and cooking the food. You can share the responsibilities when making your favorite dishes by helping each other with the cooking steps. What is most important is working together and both being equally involved. Make it special by tasting each other's recipes as they cook, and sharing ideas about what spices or ingredients to add. More essential than how the meal turns out, is the experience of creating it together in a loving way.

Set the Table

The ambiance of the dinner is just as important as how the food tastes. Work together on creating a romantic atmosphere. Start by clearing the dining table, and then place down an attractive table cloth that has a dreamy holiday design or image. Then, place on the table your best dinnerware and wine glasses. Use cloth napkins and napkin rings that are festive and pretty. Lastly, make sure to place a pair of taper candles between your place settings, and light the candles. Maybe you will also want to add some scented candles or incense in the background for a romantic aroma.

Enjoy the Special Dinner

Sit down at the table together and say a prayer for your love for each other, now and in the future. Take your time to enjoy the meal. Eat slowly, enjoy feeding each other small bites occasionally, touch hands, and converse softly about the day you met, Christmas memories you have shared, or simply what the holidays and love means to you both. Close the dinner with a kiss to show how much you appreciate each other as individuals and as a couple on this special day and always.

Exchange Gifts

The dinner may be done, but the night is far from over. Now is the time to exchange gifts if you wish. Even if your gifts are inexpensive, they can still be loving and thoughtful. Maybe you will give each other handmade cards with your own personal messages of love and joy. Or you might have purchased some personalized gifts - such as shirts, hats, coffee mugs, or pens - with festive and romantic pictures, and messages that reflect your true feelings for each other.

Christmas is not just for children; it is also a perfect time for you to show love for your significant other. Christmas dinner is the most romantic aspect of the holiday. What is mainly special about a romantic Christmas dinner is enjoying the love and togetherness that you share with your partner, and making lasting memories that you both can share for years to come.

CHAPTER 6

PSYCHOLOGY, SELF-HELP, AND VALUES

The Correlation between Low Self-Esteem and Depression

Low self-esteem is common in the world and it doesn't receive the attention it deserves. When a person has low self-esteem it affects her whole life. She often does not go to social events, does not have positive relationships, and does not feel genuinely happy. These attributes of low self-esteem can lead to depression, in which she will feel bad about her life in an all-encompassing way. The correlation between low self-esteem and depression should be analyzed in order to resolve both personal issues.

Low self-esteem is a very personal, and often private, subject for the beholder. In fact, a person who feels inadequate does not want to be noticed, because the attention makes her feel self-conscious. She would prefer to hide in a shell, so to speak, and never come out. She is often fearful of the world, because other people intimidate her.

Sometimes people with low self-esteem get picked on and that makes matters worse. The person can develop depression because of the overwhelming negative reactions from other people and the negative feelings she has about herself. According to the National Institute of Mental Health, some symptoms of depression include: feelings of persistent sadness, hopelessness, helplessness, and guilt, as well as fatigue.

It is best not to acknowledge a person's lack of confidence and instead focus on bringing out her good points, which will help raise her self-esteem. In addition, being a friend to her instead of a bully will increase her confidence. It is not helpful or admirable to bring another person down. Rather, people should "lift" each other up with positive comments to make life more enjoyable for everyone.

If low self-esteem is the cause of the depression, healing it will lessen or eliminate the depression. If the initial problem of low self-esteem improves - with the help of others as well as self-improvement techniques - the depression will lift.

The opposite can also be true - low self-esteem can be similar to a symptom of depression. In other words, having depression makes her more susceptible to having low self-esteem, likely because of low energy and negative feelings. In this situation, the depression must be treated in order for her self-esteem to improve.

Low self-esteem and depression often go hand-in-hand. However, both can be helped, and sometimes resolved, by various therapeutic methods, such as positive comments from peers, self-improvement techniques, and counseling. No one should have to live with low self-esteem or depression. Instead, the person should talk to someone she trusts about what she is going through. Once the low self-esteem and depression are cared for, she can move on with her life in a more positive light.

Sources

National Institute of Mental Health -
www.nimh.nih.gov/health/publications/men-and-depression/symptoms-of-depression-and-mania.shtml

The Difference between Introversion and Shyness

Shyness and introversion are terms that are often used interchangeably. They both reflect a reserved and quiet individual who shies away from social situations. However, the terms are different and have clearly different definitions. The most notable difference is the reason why the shy person or introvert is quiet and reserved.

An introvert would rather be alone than in a crowd. He likes to pursue solitary activities, and it does not bother him to do so. He would rather think to himself than speak out loud. When in a group of people, he will not speak up much, because he feels best when internalizing his ideas and keeping them to himself. However, if he were asked to share his ideas, he would be willing and comfortable to do so, even though he probably would not say much. He is an intellectual person who likes to contemplate and analyze things. For example, an article published on PsychologyToday.com states: "Introversion is a preference for quiet, minimally stimulating environments." In other words, introverts prefer the quiet environments that they seek.

On the other hand, "shyness is the fear of negative judgment" (Psychology Today). Therefore, people who are shy are typically afraid of what other people think of them. They try to avoid receiving negative reactions for what they say or do, and that leads them to avoid people altogether. Shy people avoid conversations and confrontations, and are afraid of embarrassment.

However, "psychologists have found that shyness and introversion do overlap....a shy person may become more introverted over time [due to shying away from social situations,] and an introvert may become shy after continually receiving the message that there's something wrong with him [for not being outgoing]" (Psychology Today). In general, society tends to shun quiet individuals and praise talkative types. In fact, "there's a shared bias in our society against [shyness and introversion]....the shy person is afraid to speak up, while the introvert is simply overstimulated - but to the outside world, the two appear to be the same, and neither type is welcome" (Psychology Today).

It is unfortunate that quiet people are looked down upon. They have just as many great ideas and thoughts that are brewing inside them from internal reflection. All they need is guidance and encouragement to deliver their insights to the world. Maybe, someday, shy people will be encouraged to share their ideas, and introverts will be valued for their wisdom and insight.

Sources

Psychology Today -
www.psychologytoday.com/blog/quiet-the-power-introverts/201107/are-you-shy-introverted-both-or-neither-and-why-does-it-matte

How Low Self-Esteem Impacts Relationships

Low self-esteem not only affects the individual but also the people around them. In fact, relationships are difficult to maintain, for a person with low self-esteem, because of their shyness and indifference. In regard to relationships, low self-esteem leads to inadequate communication, less enjoyment, and emotional distance.

Inadequate Communication

People with low self-esteem have trouble communicating because they do not feel worthy. It is very hard for them to initiate conversation, speak what is on their mind, and contribute to discussions. This lack of communication greatly affects their relationships. It is difficult for others to get close to them, because they don't speak much about their life. Some people view this shyness as indifference and apathy. Some may even think they are dishonest because they are not sharing what is on their mind. Not sharing with others can be as harmful to a relationship as sharing too much. However, by trying to open up more to others, the person with low self-esteem will likely receive positive reinforcement, which will further help their relationships.

Less Enjoyment

It is difficult to have fun around a person with low self-esteem. Their inhibited and reserved nature affects others and prevents enjoyment with others. Because they feel down about who they are, it is often hard for others to have fun with them. The person with low self-esteem has a hard time expressing enjoyment because of their solemn mood. It is helpful when other people show extra kindness to a person with low self-esteem, and point out good aspects of their personality. This helps them feel more confident. And, if others can make them laugh, their mood often improves, and the atmosphere will immediately feel more carefree.

Emotional Distance

Those who have low self-esteem are often emotionally distant from others, because they do not want anyone to notice their faults, whether real, disproportioned, or imaginary. They would rather avoid contact with people than have their shortcomings recognized. Their low self-esteem generally creates emotional distance from others. Lacking communication and enjoyment, as mentioned above, also creates emotional distance. People with low self-esteem have less relationships. Their lack of confidence prevents them from getting close to others and giving to others. When a person with low self-esteem appears apathetic in the presence of others, people think they don't like them. Improving communication - by talking more, asking questions, and offering more information - will increase self-esteem and help relationships to develop. As well, putting in effort to enjoy moments spent with others, will help establish closer relationships.

Self-Esteem and Relationships can Improve

Low self-esteem is best improved when a person focuses on their positive attributes. Eventually, they will see less negatives and will feel better about their personality. They will grow more confident, and their relationships will improve and increase in number. When a person feels better about who they are, other people will be drawn to them and they will naturally develop more meaningful relationships.

How to Break Bad Habits

Bad habits are hard to break. A habit is simply when you get so used to something that it becomes second-nature. At this point, part of the behavior is being processed in the subconscious mind. Because you're less aware of what you're doing, you have less control over it, and that makes it hard to change.

The first step to breaking a bad habit is to become conscious of it. If you usually spend too much money shopping, begin focusing on the purchases you make, paying attention to the amount of money you spend each time you buy something, and keep a mental tally of the total. Also, look over your credit card statements and take notice to how quickly purchases add up, and then think of which purchases you could live without. Once you're more aware of the damage the habit is causing you, you will have a clearer picture of what you need to do.

Next, plan out how you will break the habit. By being prepared for everything that could happen during your efforts, and determining how to deal with those situations, you will have a better chance for success. For example, if you want to cut out junk food, decide how you will go about cleaning out your kitchen of unhealthy food, what food you will have instead when you get cravings, and any positive habits, such as exercise, that you could do during times when you normally eat the most junk food.

The next step, is to change your behavior. Go about your day how you think you would without having a bad habit. You may still have a tendency to fall into old behaviors, but with conscious effort, you can choose to do something else that is more constructive. For example, if your goal is to stop biting your nails, get a manicure or give yourself one, to trim away any areas that would tempt you to bite. Also, with a manicure your nails will look nicer and that may inspire you to keep them that way. Then spend the day cleaning your home, working, or on day trips, to occupy your time as you get used to your life without the habit.

Some tips, to help your mental thought process reject the old behavior and accept the new, are: imagery and thought control. Every day, and as needed, visualize your life without the feeling of the bad habit, and then make that life a reality. If you wish to quit drinking alcohol, picture your day and night without any alcoholic beverages. Picture how you will behave and what you will do, and then behave that way and do those things. You may be pretending to be that ideal image at first, but as more sober days add up, you will eventually become that person.

Also, dismissing thoughts that could derail your efforts will help you stick to your plan. For example, if you want to quit smoking, do not think about smoking. Mentally dismiss thoughts you have about smoking and think about something else. It also helps to replace the destructive thoughts with healthy actions, like going for a walk after dinner, which was a time when you always used to smoke.

Lastly, avoid people and places that will likely bring the bad habit back into your life. For example, you should avoid the mall for a while if shopping was a problem. Or you may avoid fast food restaurants if you are trying to lose weight. Avoid bars and clubs if you are trying to stop drinking. And don't spend time with people who you used to smoke with. Stimuli for various habits are everywhere, so pick the ones that are triggers and leave them out of your life. This is especially important in the beginning, when you will be sensitive to temptations. Down the road, you might develop the ability to withstand reminders of your past self. But as a new and improved person, you may never wish to return to environments and people that involve your old, bad habit.

Your bad habit was established at one point, so it can also be removed and replaced by good behaviors. Make the decision to make a positive change, take the plunge, and stick to your intentions. A few months spent breaking a bad habit is well worth enjoying the rest of your life without it.

How to Really Listen

Listening is a communication skill that must be learned. It comes naturally to some, and others have a hard time learning to listen. Fortunately, listening skills can develop and improve. There are several techniques that make a person a great listener.

Clear Your Mind of Distractions

In order to really listen to someone, your thoughts must be clear of concerns. Temporarily set aside thoughts about daily events, struggles, triumphs, good news, bad news, and any other distractions that take your attention away from the speaker's words and message. In other words, stop thinking about your own concerns and start thinking about someone else's.

Focus Your Attention on the Speaker

Next, turn your focus entirely to the speaker. Make substantial eye contact, smile, keep your hands by your side (if standing) or placed in your lap (if sitting), and be quiet. To thoroughly listen means you have to be completely quiet while another person is talking. Forget about yourself for right now and focus all of your attention on the speaker.

Learn to Really Listen

To listen intently, you must "let go" of thoughts unrelated to the speaker's message. Try to maintain your attention the best you can by ignoring distractions, focusing on the speaker's words and message, and lessening the urge to speak by keeping the speaker's viewpoint in mind. In addition, show the speaker you are listening, through your body language, to be respectful of them and to encourage them to continue speaking. Favorable body language means facing the speaker, leaning slightly forward, maintaining natural eye contact, and nodding.

The Act of Listening

While you listen, you should take notice of things, such as the speaker's message (by putting the words together to develop a meaning or purpose), implied messages (by "reading between the lines"), and body language. By observing the speaker's body language you will be better able to provide a complementing response through your own body language, and that will help the speaker get his or her message across easier. For example, if the speaker wants to work through a difficult problem and needs you to listen for a lengthy period of time, it would help to ask probing questions to assist the person in getting through their problem more easily.

Concentration and Empathy

Effective listening takes complete concentration. It involves suppressing personal thoughts, having empathy for the speaker, and showing the speaker your empathy. With practice, people can be less concerned with themselves and become better listeners. You will find that you gain just as much from the exchange by being a good listener as you do when you are the speaker.

Negative Aspects of Dwelling on the Past

Dwelling on the past is one of the worst things a person can do. It creates worry and anxiety; leads to depression and suicide; decreases quality and length of life; and negatively affects health and wellbeing. Not to mention, it is also stressful and debilitating. These negative results of dwelling on the past are discussed below - which will hopefully help a person choose to take action to stop dwelling on the past - as well as information and guidance on how to do so.

Mental Health

Dwelling on the past, at minimum, makes a person feel sad. In some people, this sadness can manifest into clinical depression. Depression carries many symptoms, including suicidal thoughts. It is possible that if someone is so depressed about his or her past and can't let go of past hurts, he or she could become suicidal. Dwelling on the past also causes worry and nervousness in some people - which is anxiety at a more intense level - because memories of bad decisions produce bad feelings in the present.

Physical Health

Dwelling on the past takes a physical toll on the body. The excess anxiety and stress: raises blood pressure, which can lead to heart attacks and strokes; impairs the immune system, which leads to more colds and sicknesses; and causes ulcers and asthma flare-ups (Personal Stress Management). Furthermore, stress and anxiety can decrease length of life.

Emotional Health

Dwelling on the past also negatively affects emotional health, such as a person's moods, feelings, and general wellbeing. Inevitably, regret and sadness about the past lessens the quality of a person's life.

How to Stop Dwelling on the Past

The above negative results of dwelling on the past are reason enough, as well as motivation, to learn how to stop thinking, and viewing life, that way. For some people, it may take prayer, meditation, or counseling to overcome bad feelings about the past, but it is possible.

A person should attempt to let go of the past by forgiving him- or herself and others; accepting past circumstances, by deciding to move on with his or her life; and lastly, appreciating the goodness in the present. In addition, affirmative self-talk can help a person train him- or herself to let go of debilitating thoughts about the past and live in the present.

It is so important for people to not live in the past or let it bring them down. Life is much easier to deal with when burdens of the past are forgotten and focus is turned toward the present. People have less worry, stress, sickness, sadness if they live in the present moment, by taking life moment by moment. Letting go of the past will make a person feel "lighter" and is well worth the effort.

Sources

Personal Stress Management -
www.personal-stress-management.com/stress-related-diseases.html

The Relationship between Willpower and Procrastination

Willpower helps to deter procrastination. In fact, if you maintain it, willpower will keep you from procrastinating, forever. It is very interesting how the two terms work, and how they work together.

Willpower, simply stated, is the desire to do something. Willpower is felt when you want to start a task. When you want to act, willpower is what is fueling your desire. It is easy to complete a project when you have the willpower to do it. However, in order to finish a task, you must maintain your willpower throughout the entire process. That is because acting on something is near impossible if you don't want to.

Furthermore, sustained willpower can prevent procrastination from happening at all. Procrastination is when you delay an action for some reason. You may even come up with several justifications as to why you need to delay the project, and then you may confirm that you will do it later. Sometimes, something else takes precedence at the moment. Regardless, the action is postponed because it is not favorable.

You can probably think of many reasons why you cannot do something that you don't like to do. Oftentimes, the task is delayed longer than ideal. This is simply from not having the willpower to do it because you postponed the task, and in doing so, you also postponed the drive to do it.

However, keeping willpower up will combat procrastination. But, how do you maintain a steady flow of willpower all the time? The answer is, not to lose sight of the prize. By focusing on your destination, and not spending much time thinking about how far you've come, you will always have the will to accomplish more. Do not stop short of your goals to congratulate yourself, because your willpower will interpret this brief rest as completion. When that happens, it does not desire to accomplish any more. Willpower must be fed continuously, or else is dies out.

Therefore, in order to maintain willpower, it is best to have a goal to focus on at all times. You may even want to have goals planned out in advance, for when you complete previous goals. Simple goals, like getting the dishes done every day, will maintain the flow of will. Sound tiring? It really isn't, because if you think about it, most people usually accomplish something every day, and if you have the will to do it, it makes it easier.

If you always have willpower, by focusing on your goals, there will be no opportunities for procrastination. To accomplish your goals, it is therefore best to not look back, but to keep moving forward.

Schizoaffective Disorder: Two Illnesses in One Diagnosis

Schizoaffective disorder is a mental illness categorized under schizophrenia. It involves two parts:

1. A mood component - either bipolar (mania and depression) or depression alone.
2. Psychosis (what people with schizophrenia experience).

Because of these two parts, treatment is multifaceted and managing the illness is challenging. It is important for the person with schizoaffective disorder, as well as his close friends and family, to understand the different parts of the disorder, in order to assist with treatment and management of the illness, along with establishing healthier existences and relationships.

The first part, psychosis, can involve several symptoms: delusions (believing things that aren't true), hallucinations (experiencing sensations that aren't real), disorganized thinking, odd or unusual behavior, slow movements, lack of emotional expression in the face and voice, low motivation, and difficulty communicating (MedicineNet). The person with schizoaffective disorder can have some or all of these symptoms. Because his reality is distorted, it is very difficult for him to function and work.

The second part, is depressive symptoms, whether in combination with mania or alone. Depressive symptoms are debilitating; they include: lack of (or increased) appetite, weight loss or gain, changes in typical sleep patterns, restlessness or agitation, low energy, disinterest in usual activities, feeling worthless or hopeless, guilt, inability to think clearly, and suicidal thoughts (MedicineNet). Depressive symptoms are difficult to tolerate, but they can be treated with a combination of medication and therapy, which will lift the person's depressed mood.

Mania sometimes accompanies depression for people with schizoaffective disorder. Mania is at the opposite end of depression, and symptoms include: increased activity (work, social, or sexual), talking more than usual, racing thoughts, less need for sleep, agitation, increased self-confidence, easily distracted, and excessive and destructive behavior (MedicineNet). When manic, sometimes people can stay awake for long periods, spend more money than they can afford, or drive unsafely. Like psychotic and depressive symptoms, people with mania have a distorted perception. Sometimes they end up dealing with the consequences of their behavior after the manic episode, or they can quickly fall into depression. When mania and depression are the combined mood component, the person can get tossed between the manic highs and the depressive lows in a short time, causing each mood state to feel even more extreme.

Schizoaffective disorder is a serious mental illness that needs to be treated by a psychiatrist. It is also helpful for the person to see a psychologist to help talk through daily or weekly struggles. People with schizoaffective disorder do not have to remain isolated, because there is help out in the world. The more informed the family and friends are about the person's illness, the more supportive and helpful they can be. The person with schizoaffective should also educate himself about his condition, because with a greater understanding, therapeutic techniques will be more effective. It is also essential for him to keep his doctors updated on what he is experiencing for more improved treatment. With all of these options available, the person with schizoaffective can live a more normal and positive life.

Sources

MedicineNet -
www.medicinenet.com/schizoaffective_disorder/article.htm

Symptoms of Emotional Abuse

It is sometimes difficult to tell if someone is being emotional abused because the signs are subtle when compared to other types of abuse. For example, there is no physical evidence; the bruises, scars, and damage is internal. The way to tell if someone is being emotionally abused, is through the person's personality and the way they act around others. By reading the symptoms below, you will be more able to recognize emotional abuse in others, or even yourself.

A "Down" Personality

An emotionally abused person experiences depression or periods of sadness that may be prolonged. These feelings show on the outside as a person who is serious and gloomy. The person may or may not be this way all the time, because some people are able to hide their true feelings well.

Timid, Shy, Repressed, or Passive

People who don't express themselves or their needs to others are afraid of what people will think of them. This is typical behavior of people who are emotionally abused, because they want and try to avoid conflict, probably since there is fighting at home.

Sensitive or Frightened Easily

Individuals who are overly sensitive to other people's comments; those who exhibit fear from others' dominant personalities; those who back down from discussions; and those who avoid confrontations or debates, might be receiving emotional abuse from someone. The person generally "runs" from aggressive situations and individuals.

A "People Pleaser"

In this case, "people pleasing" is not something to make fun of or look down upon. People pleasers wish to satisfy others' needs, because they receive positive reinforcement in return. Receiving positive reinforcement is the opposite of being emotionally abused.

Emotionally Abusive to Others

On the other hand, a certain number of recipients of emotional abuse act out their pain by being emotionally abusive to others. These people emulate what is being done to them as a way to ease their hurt, or because they cannot help but do to others what is being done to them. For instance, being emotionally abusive is how they were "taught" to treat others, so that is how they behave.

However, being emotionally abusive to others is not the right way to deal with received emotional abuse. The proper outlet and solution is through family counseling or individual therapy (preferably both). Group therapy, or support groups, may also be helpful, especially for individuals who are more expressive of their thoughts and feelings.

It is best for those who are emotionally abused to get away from their abuser as soon as possible. The victims should find supportive and loving living situations and relationships. The emotionally abused do not deserve the abuse they receive. The abuser is the one who is wrong.

Why Etiquette is Important

Having etiquette involves acting a certain way. Politeness, tactfulness, and empathy are forms of etiquette. Etiquette is also a reflection of character that shows selflessness and consideration for others. It is important to use etiquette for the following situations.

In Communication

When communicating, etiquette means being respectful of others. It means you listen intently when people speak, and you volunteer information without interrupting others. It also means being courteous, by making comfortable eye contact, saying 'please' and 'thank you,' and asking questions. All of these characteristics show you are interested in, and respectful of, your companions and acquaintances. Good etiquette in communication also involves having compassion for people. To show true compassion, imagine what it is like to actually be the person that you are with, then keep that perspective in mind when you speak and act. That is showing empathy, which is a part of having etiquette. Remember to treat people how you want to be treated. Having etiquette in conversation is essentially being respectful of your peers by using appropriate communication skills and manners.

With New Acquaintances

It is important to demonstrate etiquette behavior all of the time, but this is especially true with new acquaintances. You should tread lightly (not be "overpowering") upon your first few encounters with a new acquaintance. First impressions are important for developing relationships which is why it is admirable to be polite and respectful, especially with new acquaintances. To start with, a 'hello,' a smile, and a handshake are good practices of etiquette. Maybe you will see the person again, and maybe it will develop into a friendship or relationship of some sort. Since you never know, it is best to play it safe by showing your best behavior.

Additional Thoughts and Advice about Etiquette

Proper etiquette is a valuable skill to have. Fortunately, it can be learned and taught to others. Having etiquette requires slowing down your actions to become more aware of your behavior and speech. Demonstrating etiquette shows that you have respect for yourself and others; you care about appropriateness and tactful behavior; you have a good sense of what is right and wrong; and you have priorities, values, and self-esteem. By being polite, tactful, and empathetic, you make people feel comfortable, and this reflects that you have a high regard for life. If everyone used etiquette the world would be a more civil and enjoyable place.

Why Many Women Have a Negative Body Image

Body image is the way a person views their body. It can be realistic or unrealistic. It affects how a person "feels" in their body. For example, when not looking in a mirror, people have a sense of what their body looks like. Positive body image is having a realistic and accepting view of your body. However, very few women have a positive body image. Society, dieting, eating disorders, and obesity are all related to a negative body image.

A century ago, full and curvaceous bodies were admired. They were also more natural for women to maintain. Nowadays, the ideal female body has a tiny waist, flat stomach, thin thighs, and is very slim. Women are subliminally told to weigh less than ever before. Supermodels are the new women idols. However, most of them are preteens or teenagers, and many of them have eating disorders or diet strictly. Trying to live up to these standards is hard on most women. As a result, they starve themselves, or exercise excessively, or both.

Body mass index (BMI) charts are not realistic for everyone. BMI charts do not consider bone structure, muscle mass, figure, or genes. Studies have been conducted revealing that people in the overweight category actually have *less* health problems than those in the normal category. Because the normal category is unreachable for many women, these weight charts— which are supposed to help with setting healthy weight goals—are actually harmful to women's health.

Most women that are aware of the standard of beauty and body weight are dieting to reduce and change their figures. This can lead to self-starvation, excessive exercise, bingeing and purging, or all three. Eating disorders are not simply unhealthy diet habits; they are categorized as mental illnesses and can sometimes end in death. Strict dieting or food restriction, combined with a negative or distorted body image, can become an eating disorder.

A negative body image can also lead to obesity. This is due to excessive eating to soothe and comfort bad feelings about their bodies (and selves). In addition, yo-yo dieting, which often accompanies negative body image, leads to increasingly higher weights with each diet attempt.

A negative body image is detrimental to women. It may help to see a counselor that specializes in treating women with negative body images. Lastly, if society worked on promoting healthy lifestyles and healthy looking bodies for women, a lot of good would come from it.

CHAPTER 7

WRITING

Challenges for the Freelance Writer

Freelance writing is a rewarding career. You can work from home and arrange your schedule to meet your needs. However, there are several challenges that go along with being a freelance writer: initial low pay, hard work, and less social life. By being aware of these challenges, you will get through them and succeed at your career.

Initial Low Pay

Freelance writing is a slow-starting career, income-wise. It takes time - at least months, and often years - to establish a writing portfolio and get substantial work published, in order to earn enough income to support yourself. Websites that pay their freelance writers based on page views or revenue share often start at pennies a day for an article. So, initially, you will not make enough money to live comfortably.

However, if you save money prior to becoming a freelance writer, you can supplement your income until you can support yourself on your writing alone. And if you put enough effort into the quality and quantity of your writing pieces, your income will increase at an even faster rate. Months or years down the road, you may even surprise yourself as to how much you can earn as a freelance writer.

Hard Work

Producing lots of quality writing and promoting it is hard work. Often, the effort put forth drains your energy because writing takes a lot of concentration and time, no matter how talented at writing you are. Since you work from home, incorporating family, household duties, and distractions into the job makes freelance writing quite a challenge.

However, there is good news. Writing, revising, and publishing gets easier with practice. And the longer you continue with freelance writing, the more skilled you will be at juggling life responsibilities and managing your time. So by sticking with the career, by continuing to hone your craft, freelance writing will become easier, and the stress will lessen.

Less Social Life

Freelance writers spend a lot of their waking hours at home typing, researching, writing, editing, and publishing. These are typically solitary activities that take time and focus. Therefore, you will not interact with others as much as with more social-orientated careers. Plus, by working at home, it is often easy to work more hours than average and spend less time with friends and family.

But if you enjoy doing creative activities independently, having less of a social life won't bother you. You may enjoy the quiet time spent doing something you love that is personally and professionally rewarding. In addition, like stated previously, the longer you are a freelance writer, the more free time you will acquire as you get skilled at your career, so you will have increasingly more time to spend with important people in your life.

Struggling Initially Will Pay Off in the Future

As a freelance writer, you will struggle most when first starting out. Then your career will likely pick up and you will have more money, energy, and free time which is ultimately the main goal - and perk - of being a freelance writer.

The Differences between a Newspaper Editor and a Book Editor

Newspaper editors and book editors are both involved with the editing process of written materials. They have deadlines and variety in their jobs. However, there are clear differences between the two occupations that are important to know.

General Job Description of a Newspaper Editor

Newspaper editors oversee the production of a newspaper. They decide what news will be in the paper, assign news stories to reporters, edit articles, and sometimes write articles. They influence the layout of the newspaper, which includes where the articles will be featured and the positioning of the ads.

Types of Newspaper Editors

There are various types of newspaper editors depending on the size of the newspaper and the frequency of publication.

- Managing editors receive news stories, determine the worthiness, and assign them to the reporters. They also help determine the newspaper layout.
- Story editors receive national interest news and photographs from news services and decide what to do with it, such as assign it to the front page or adjust the size.
- Copy editors correct mistakes in the articles and arrange them to fit the newspaper's format.

- Makeup editors decide how the newspaper will look with help from the managing editor. They decide how the ads and articles will be arranged, as well as how many of each for every page. If a newspaper is published multiple times in a day, they will redesign the pages as new news comes in.
- Associate editors cover two or more paper sections for small, weekly newspapers.

Other editors are responsible for articles based on location; for example, municipal, suburban, or regional types of articles. Some are assigned to the different sections of the paper, such as sport editor, art editor, or business editor.

Working Conditions of a Newspaper Editor

Newspaper editors work long days and have irregular hours because of not knowing when a big news story will come in. Their jobs are high-pressure because of continuous, ongoing deadlines. They have a lot of responsibility, because readers expect the facts to be right, and because they are generally responsible for the content of the newspaper. However, every day is different and that can be exciting.

Career Life as a Book Editor

Book editors work at publishing houses and deal with many parts of the publishing process. They make corrections on authors' books while taking into consideration the audience and genre. In regards to audience, book editors keep in mind society's current interests, as well as make sure the language is congruent with modern times. They have tight deadlines to keep the books from becoming outdated.

Book editors have to consider the future of the book, such as a possible movie productions, sequels, and so forth. Their main purpose is to create a polished product and that involves working with cover designers and production. They also help with book promotion after publication.

Fortunately, book editors only need to be familiar with the editing and publishing process of the types of books their publishing house publishes. As well, many book editors specialize in certain types of books and certain genres. And they often have an assistant to help with proofreading, checking facts, and other supportive tasks.

Most of a book editor's time is spent reading and correcting manuscripts. They work closely with authors to create the best product for readers. Book editors must maintain tactfulness when editing books in order to have professional and satisfactory relationships with the authors.

Types of Book Editors

Because a lot of work goes into preparing a book for publication, there are several types of book editors to handle the different tasks.

- Managing editors manage the finances and budget related to book production. They also track deadlines from a financial perspective.
- Executive editors decide what books the publishing house will work with based on their budget and

marketing trends. They decide how many copies of each published book are needed and handle reprint orders.

- Editor-in-chief is the highest-ranking editor in a publishing house. They oversee the editorial department and makes sure there is adequate business to support the publishing house's budget.
- Acquisitions editors do research to seek out new authors and books. They negotiate with authors on movie and reprint sales. They also campaign books, and follow trends in reading.
- Production editors are responsible for the production and manufacturing of books.
- Copy editors review manuscripts to correct errors and improve style.
- Rights and permissions editors prepare samples of books to submit to book clubs. They research costs of artists' and photographers' illustrations. And they obtain legal permission for using quotes.

Making a Choice

Clearly, newspaper editors and book editors are very different occupations. The type of work and nature of the work is different for each. There should now be an understanding of what the two careers are like so that choosing a path will be a more educated and knowledgeable decision.

Sources

State University -
http://careers.stateuniversity.com/pages/122/Editor-Newspaper.html

State University -
http://careers.stateuniversity.com/pages/119/Editor-Book.html

How to Overcome Writer's Block

All writers experience a slump of ideas occasionally. You will sit down to write but will draw a blank. Try as you might, nothing will surface. Or you will start writing, but not many words come to mind, or your ideas don't seem worthwhile enough to write about. You may have a professional, educational, or personal writing responsibility but can't get started or finished. The information below will help you tackle those times when you have writer's block.

First of all, do not accept that you have writer's block. It is only real if you believe in it, so don't put yourself through that negativity. Believing you have writer's block will hinder your thought process and creative ideas even more. Ignore the term "writer's block" and any disabling thoughts associated with it. Also overlook the desire to feel sad or mad, because those feelings don't help ideas surface. Ideas and creativity flow best with a positive outlook.

Next, try doing something besides writing to give your mind a break. Pick up a book and read about topics that interest you. Reading is a way to be involved in writers' activities without actually writing. Reading will help improve your writing skills and vocabulary for when you get back to it. It is a great way to relax and feel positive. Another plus is that reading will stimulate your subconscious mind, which can lead to writing ideas.

You can also try activities that are not at all related to writing, like taking a nap, going for a walk, working out, doing housework, drawing or painting, or taking photography to allow room for more ideas.

Another effective technique is talking to supportive and positive people. These people could be writers, non-writers, friends, family, coworkers, colleagues, therapists, or acquaintances. Choose people you are close to for personal advice and those you are not as close to, or professionals, for objective advice. Tell them about your frustration and disappointment. Explain what you are going through. Share your hopes and aspirations. Try bouncing ideas off them. At the least, they can offer a supportive hug and wish you the best.

Now is the time to dip your toes in the writing fountain. Start by writing simple journal entries, a short poem, or a list of ideas and things you wish to accomplish. You could then try doing preliminary research if that is your style. The writing, brainstorming, and research will typically stir up some ideas, maybe more than you imagined. This is because your mind had a chance to acquire and formulate ideas while it was resting. Save some ideas from your lists for other days. Occasional brainstorming is a great way to avoid writer's block in the future.

Now that you have topics and some preliminary writing done, the serious writing begins. Make your way back to the computer and write what feels natural. You will likely be happy to be back to productive writing. Use your notes, lists, research, and journal to refer to as needed to stimulate your writing "juices."

You are officially back to your craft. Congratulations on getting through your idea slump. Your "writer's block" is now over. It will probably return someday, but next time you will know what to do and will feel more confident that you can tackle it.

How to Start a Career as a Freelance Writer

Freelance writing is an enjoyable career, especially for those who love to write. It is also a slow-starting career, because the income is usually low at first and it takes time to build. Therefore, being a freelance writer involves a lot of hard work and planning. But, if you write well, you will gain credibility and clients, and the money will eventually fall into place.

The first thing to do, even before you've cleared your schedule for freelance writing, is to have a reserve of money set aside to supplement your income during the first few months. This will allow you to have time to develop your career. It takes about six months to get used to a freelance writing schedule, have substantial published writing to earn from, and establish yourself as a published writer. With money set aside, you will be less stressed about bills and expenses while you are establishing your new career.

Begin writing right away. You should write every day to build up your portfolio. You get paid for the writing you do, so the more you write, the more you will make. Also, write the best you can in a reasonable amount of time. Quality is just as important as quantity, but you must also set limits on the amount of time you will allow yourself to spend on each writing project, in order to maintain your desired hourly rate.

Begin looking for writing websites that will pay you to write for them and publish your work on those websites. You will soon find out the best websites, depending on your needs and what styles you prefer. You can write for one, or many, websites. Also look for websites that will connect you to clients who need written material, and apply for the projects. You should also search websites that post regular jobs for freelance writers, and apply to them.

Take each job application seriously. Show the client your best work - based on the type of job - and format your resume and cover letter according to each job you apply to. Clients look to hire freelance writers that write well and can meet deadlines. Highlight your strengths and abilities, and represent yourself and your work well. You will get more, long-lasting job opportunities this way.

It is imperative to have a "system" that you follow every day. It doesn't have to be an organized schedule - even though they do help for some people. Vitally, it should be your own method of productivity that helps you stay focused and get work done on a regular basis. The most important thing about a system, is that it works well for you.

You will probably notice that the workload and effort involved with freelance writing will get easier as time passes. This is because your writing and freelancing skills will improve, and you will establish yourself as a freelance writer. This is good news, and it's your reward for a successful start as a freelance writer.

Techniques Employed by a Good Writer

Some writers are naturally creative; but good writing skills are developed through education, experience, and effort. There are certain writing techniques that are employed by a good writer. If these techniques are practiced enough, a writer will develop the ability to write well. The following is a list of techniques that good writers demonstrate.

Organized Prose

Organized writing is easy to follow and enjoyable to read. At minimum, organized prose has an introduction, body, and conclusion. Usually there is a thesis statement or topic sentence. Often there is more than one point made in the body of the written work. Regardless, all good writers introduce, share, and close in their writing.

Clear and Concise Content

Good writers write clearly and concisely by expressing the point and purpose of their message with accurate words and by using as few words as possible. Good writers do not confuse their readers with unnecessary words, because it makes the meaning unclear and hard to follow. Less "fluff" and stronger words creates more vivid imagery and greater understanding by readers.

Varied Word Usage

A thesaurus is a good writer's best friend. Varying the words used in a piece of writing is important because it makes the piece interesting. On the other hand, when the same few words are repeated too many times in a written work, the writing sounds repetitive and lacks authority.

Varied Sentence Structure

The way the sentences are put together should vary as well. Mix short and long sentences; and change up the clauses and phrases within sentences by using different independent and dependent clauses, and prepositional phrases. Variety in sentence structure makes the written work interesting and enjoyable to read.

Parallelism

In other circumstances, parallelism in writing is important. Parallelism means creating sentence phrases and clauses that follow the same structure. This is important when listing items between commas and semicolons. When clauses and phrases are parallel, readers can comprehend the meaning and organization of the sentence better. In addition, words in a list should be parallel too. For example, in most cases a good writer keeps the word tense (past, present, or future) the same throughout the written work. Also, the type of word (noun, verb, adjective, or adverb) should remain constant in a list of items in a sentence.

Keeps the Reader's Interest

It is very important for writers to keep their readers' interest or else they will lose readers, because the readers will stop buying the writer's books. Losing readers is a writer's worst fear; after all, the biggest reward of being a writer is when readers appreciate their work. Not having readers is similar to an employee doing all sorts of work for a company that doesn't exist.

Writes Appropriately for the Medium

Blog posts are different from novels; articles are different from poems; and short stories are different from technical reports. As well, fiction is different than nonfiction, and creative writing is different than technical writing. Therefore, the style and formatting of a written piece should be different based on the type of writing. Good writers keep the intended medium in mind when they write, and in turn, the writing turns out better and more appropriate.

Has a Unique Writer's Voice

Writers are people, and since no two people are the same, no two writers' voices should be the same. In fact, it is refreshing for a person to read their favorite writer's work, because the reader can recognize the writer's individual voice. It is important for good writers to use their own unique voices in order to stand out from the crowd.

Uses Effective Beginnings and Endings

Good writers always begin by "hooking" the reader; then, a topic statement usually follows. That is the proper organization of a beginning, because the writer must get the reader's attention first, and then establish credibility and explain the topic. In addition, all good writing has a valid conclusion that wraps up the writing piece and gives a sense of closure.

All good writers use the above techniques, and they apply them consistently throughout each and every written work. By also being interesting, organized, direct, and appropriate, good writers are being supportive of their readership. And having readers is really what being a good writer is all about.

Christine Rice

The Top 3 Qualities of a Successful Freelance Writer

There are many successful freelance writers. However, there is a reason why they are successful, and that is because they have certain qualities that make their business lucrative and satisfying. The top three attributes a successful freelance writer possesses are: passion, productivity, and persistence.

Have a Passion for Writing

The most successful entrepreneurs are those that are infatuated with what they do. They enjoy the tasks of the job, and they don't mind working long hours because it's like a hobby to them. When freelance writers have this type of passion about writing, motivation comes easily and naturally, stemmed from a love for writing. They don't have to force themselves to accomplish work, because they *want* to work. With a passion for writing, everything about the freelance writing business becomes easier.

Enjoy Writing Large Quantities

With freelance writing, more production **always** leads to more profit. And because writing never goes to waste (there is always *somewhere* it can be published, even if it's on a personal blog), writing a ton is a good way to succeed at freelance writing. In order to be productive, a successful freelance writer writes every chance they can get. They keep a notebook on them wherever they go for when new ideas hit them. They don't miss out on any new ideas, and that makes their business thrive.

Are Persistent

Persistence leads to greater personal and financial success. This is especially true for a freelance writer, because publishing is competitive. Successful freelance writers keep applying and submitting to publishers and clients, even if they get rejections, and *especially* if they get rejections. They are always on the lookout for new writing gigs to apply to. They keep applying and submitting, because the work they do is what keeps their business successful.

Success is Within Reach

Freelance writing is hard work, especially for those who want to become successful and maintain that success. But, with the right perspective and effort, a freelance writer has the ability to succeed. Developing the qualities above will make a freelance writer successful.

Afterword

I hope you enjoyed the articles in this book. My hope is that some of the information you read will in some way help you to improve your life, even if to just make you aware of something you didn't know before.

We all have valuable knowledge and life experiences that people should know about. It is my wish that you will recommend this book to others so that they too can benefit from the advice contained within these pages. It is also my wish that you will write your own book of articles, tips, or advice about what you know about the world.

If you found this book helpful, I would be honored if you'd write a review for it. I read all of my reviews and I appreciate them all. You can also email me at christine@christinerice-author.com and let me know what you think about this book. I would love to hear from you.

In addition, if you enjoyed this book, I hope you will check out my other books:

Poetry for the Heart
Essays for the Soul
My Not-So-Ordinary Life
Freelance Writing Guide

Thank you for reading *Articles for the Mind* and I hope you enjoy my other books.

Best wishes,

Christine

About the Author

Christine Rice is a multi-published author who greatly enjoys sharing her life through her books. She has published five books: Poetry for the Heart, Essays for the Soul, My Not-So-Ordinary Life, Freelance Writing Guide, and Articles for the Mind. She is currently working on three more books: Chronicles of a Troubled Girl, Freedom from Fat, and Adolescent Angst.

When she's not working on her books, Christine helps other authors and writers publish works of their own. She owns and runs a publishing services business where she provides writing, editing, formatting, and graphic designing services.

Christine was born and raised - and currently lives - in New England with her husband and their cat. She enjoys writing, reading, shopping, movies, cafes, and dining out. She also lives a healthy lifestyle that includes healthy eating and regular exercise.

You can learn more about Christine and her books at the following locations:

Website: www.christinerice-author.com
Facebook:
www.facebook.com/christinerice.professionalwriter
Twitter: www.twitter.com/criceauthor
Goodreads: www.goodreads.com/christine_rice

www.ingramcontent.com/pod-product-compliance
Lightning Source LLC
Chambersburg PA
CBHW070901290526
45795CB00001B/201